TX   1

Southern Christian University Library
1200 Taylor Rd.
Montgomery, AL. 36117

David C. Cook Foundation Monographs
C. Lawrence Brook, Editor

This monograph series is intended for communicators involved in media worldwide. The series addresses various facets of communication, cross-cultural research, and issues related to publishing and other media. For more information, write to: Editor, David C. Cook Foundation Monographs, Cook Square, Elgin, Illinois 60120, USA.

Still in Print

Journey of a writer, teacher, journalist

Roland E. Wolseley

00030486

PN
4874
.W688
A37
1985

 David C. Cook Foundation   Elgin, Illinois USA

© 1985 Roland E. Wolseley. All rights reserved. Except for brief excerpts for review purposes, no part of this book may be reproduced in any form without written permission from the David C. Cook Foundation.

Printed in the United States of America

Designed by Betty Chu

Library of Congress Cataloging in Publication Data

Wolseley, Roland Edgar, 1904-
  Still in print.

  (David C. Cook Foundation monographs)
  Includes index.
  1. Wolseley, Roland Edgar, 1904-
2. Journalists – United States – Biography. 3. College teachers – New York (State) – Biography. 4. Syracuse University – Faculty – Biography. 5. Journalism – Study and teaching – New York (State) – Syracuse. 6. Journalism, Religious – United States. I. Title. II. Series.
PN4874.W688A37 1985   070'.92'4 [B]   84-63118
ISBN 0-89191-980-5 (pbk.)
ISBN 0-89191-311-4 (lib. bdg.)

Printed in the United States of America

To my wife, Isabel

Contents

Foreword

A good teacher inspires and motivates his students to academic excellence; but a great teacher goes beyond that by giving the student a piece of himself, a lifelong quest for learning, and the vision to become all that God intended him to be.

Roland E. Wolseley was such a teacher.

My relationship with Professor Wolseley began through an exchange of correspondence as I contemplated graduate school. During this period I was struggling with the decision whether to attend Syracuse or some other well-known journalism school— such as Northwestern University or Columbia University. He became my counselor through a series of letters, as he advised me on the strengths and weaknesses of each institution.

As a prospective student, I was impressed by his care and concern for my vocational well-being. Looking back, I'm amazed that someone in his position would have taken the time and effort to go through such a long correspondence on "speculation." However, it was precisely this personal touch that convinced me to attend Syracuse University and to pursue a graduate degree in journalism—but more important was the opportunity to meet this unusual man and study under his leadership.

As I reflect back upon those student days, I remember Professor Wolseley as a teacher, a friend, and a communicator of the Christian faith.

He is first and foremost a teacher. His love of students transcends everything else. I know that even in retirement he still is teaching someone, somewhere. While not a flashy or dynamic person in the classroom, he had an innate ability to take a student's curiosity and imagination and turn these into a lifetime of learning.

I remember the care with which he taught writing and editing. For the student's benefit he line edited every piece of writing, every news story, and every memo that crossed his desk.

One of my favorite stories occurred after I left the university. Immediately after graduation I took an editorial position with *The Upper Room*. My wife and I moved midterm, before I received confirmation of my degree. After a respectable period of time I wrote to Dr. Wolseley inquiring whether I had, in fact, graduated. His reply to my question was brief, stating that I had passed the comprehensive exams and would be receiving my diploma within a few weeks. The rest of his letter was devoted to line editing *my* letter, with the admonition that a recent graduate with two master's degrees certainly should take more care in constructing and writing a simple piece of correspondence. I've never forgotten that lesson.

During those student days Professor Wolseley and his first wife, Bernice, became surrogate parents to many of us who were so far from our own families. We spent many hours with them as they opened their lives and home to us. Always a friend to students, Dr. Wolseley became an even greater friend to graduates as he followed their careers and vocational accomplishments.

I also remember Professor Wolseley as a communicator of the faith. My wife and I were making our first visit to Syracuse the day Martin Luther King, Jr., was assassinated. As a young minister, I was deeply saddened by that event. I was a child of the sixties, with all of the unfulfilled hopes and dreams of a more just society. In Professor Wolseley I found a man of compassion, one who reached out to others regardless of background or color. In him I discovered a man of deep religious convictions and an active social conscience. Certainly among his greatest accomplishments will be the special care he gave to missionaries and future journalists who took their academic training under his tutelage. These students, in turn, took the love of learning and the inspiration provided by Dr. Wolseley around the world.

RONALD P. PATTERSON
Vice President/Director of Publishing
Abingdon Press
Nashville, Tennessee

Southern Christian University Library

Preface

Few autobiographical books of any degree of thoroughness have been written by teachers of journalism. The same can be said of books by persons identified with the journalism of religion.

There is a niche, therefore, for such a book as this one, though, like others, it makes no pretense at being fully autobiographical. It can be considered only as a portion of the full story.

The editors of the monograph series were the ones who suggested its emphasis. Through a series of conversations, including a visit to my home, they explained what they wanted: a personal monograph focusing on key experiences and people that helped shape my life as a communicator. Their purpose was to have, in writing, reflections from one who as "journalist, writer, educator, and churchman, uses journalism for a good cause."

I have tried to fulfill this purpose. Beginning with events that led to the religion journalism program at Syracuse University, I then drop back to examine earlier years. After that, I move on to other episodes that stand out in my mind—my year at Nagpur University in India, the development of black journalism courses at Syracuse, and further teaching and writing. Woven throughout the narrative are my observations and analysis of activities related to journalism, education, writing, and the teaching of writing.

If I have not carried out the intended purpose, it is my fault, for the road to be traveled was made clear enough. What I have actually done in my career may not add up to what those around me think I have done.

As I look at what I have written, the thread that holds much of it together is the fate common to so many in journalism anywhere in the world: the loneliness of the writer's occupation. If my literary and journalistic friends are any clue, there are many of us on this globe who must absorb loneliness every day. Those who can convert it into rewarding solitude are fortunate.

It is customary in prefaces to thank those who helped bring a book to reality. My principal debt is to C. Lawrence Brook, editor of the David C. Cook Foundation Monograph series, for the clarity of his direction and his painstaking suggestions for enrichment of the manuscript.

ROLAND E. WOLSELEY

Syracuse, New York
January 1985

1 New Paths at Syracuse

Creating a magazine department.
New programs in religion journalism
and literacy journalism—the rationale,
decisions to make, results.

A visitor to the Newhouse School of Public Communications at Syracuse University was sauntering one day along the faculty office corridors. He was a widely known teacher of journalism at another university.

When he reached my office door he saw over it this sign:

MAGAZINE DEPARTMENT
Literacy Journalism Program
Religious Journalism Program[1]

"Religious journalism?" I heard him exclaim in astonishment. "What in the world is that?"

I opened my door, and since we were slightly acquainted from journalism teachers' annual conventions, invited him in to explain. How much I enlightened him, if at all, I do not know.

---

1. The term was later changed to religion journalism, which covers the journalism about religion. Religious journalism is an impossibility and is mistakenly used for religion journalism. Journalism cannot have the inherent quality of being religious. Similarly, it is music journalism, not musical journalism.

Now, years later, it still is necessary to define this discipline of writing about religion for the media.

What so many strangers to this form of writing do not know is that there has been a close relationship between writing and religion for centuries. Early writing was done largely in the interest of religion, and, in the West, the church was the educational bulwark of the times. Later the tools were held by clergy alone. As late as the seventeenth century even kings and emperors often were illiterate.

It seems all the more strange, then, that writing about religion as a whole never has regained the eminent place it once occupied. While more books about religion are published than on almost any other subject and many have high sales, few have won critical respect. Thus it is with the newspapers and magazines of religion: they are many but appear to have little influence on public thinking and policy.

Analyzing and explaining this situation would fill another book elaborating a major explanation: the literary and journalistic standards of the writers, editors, and publishers of religion writing are too low. Certainly there are exceptions. They stand out because they are so far superior to the bulk of the output. How I arrived at this conclusion and what I have tried to do to improve the situation will be clearer as my own story moves along.

One of the new 500

I was one of the nearly 500 newly hired teachers in the fall of 1946 when I arrived on the campus of Syracuse University, Syracuse, New York. Colleges and universities across the USA were so overwhelmed by returning GI's that new faculty were hired in great numbers. Before Mrs. Wolseley and I left Evanston, where I had been on the faculty of the Medill School of Journalism at Northwestern University, the understanding was that in Syracuse we would be assigned to a Quonset hut in the university's colony of such buildings. Hundreds of students and faculty were accommodated on arrival. But not all. We were among those not provided for. We lived for three weeks in different hotels before moving, along with nine others, into a university-owned house. In early spring we purchased our own home only a half-dozen blocks from the School of Journalism, which occupied a castle.

Literally. Yates Castle. Some wealthy Syracusan had had it built in imitation of a Rhine River castle, moat included, although by the time I arrived on the faculty the moat had been filled. My second-floor office overlooked the Delaware, Lackawanna & Western Railway line, known for its name train, "Phoebe Snow." But much of the traffic was freight, with many open coal, cinder, and sand cars clanking by day and night. Dust and film piled in layers on my window sills, desk, books, and floor. They penetrated the books that lined the office until I was able to move them to our house.

The old castle was picturesque, not a doubt about that. Its grand stairway from the first to the second floors led to a floor-to-ceiling mirror imported from Italy. That was the building's only virtue. Floors creaked, walls were cracked, and in summer the place was roasting hot. Yet students and faculty were sentimental about Yates. Alums of the time still speak of it fondly, never having had to spend all day five or six days a week in it.[2]

Mathew Lyle Spencer and associates

The Syracuse journalism faculty I was joining had several outstanding members, led by its first dean, Mathew Lyle Spencer. Dr. Spencer was a son of a Kentucky preacher, a fact that was to be important in the launching of a religion journalism program. Two of his textbooks were among the earliest on USA journalism. International recognition came to him when he was asked to set up a journalism program for American University in Cairo, Egypt, as well as to go to Japan as a consultant on journalism education.[3]

Another widely known teacher on the Syracuse staff was Laurence R. Campbell whose specialty was scholastic journal-

2. As the castle became inadequate, the School of Journalism, founded in 1933, but for a decade before that a department of the business school, was moved elsewhere. Finally in 1962, a huge gift was received from Samuel I. Newhouse, a multimillionaire American communications magnate who owned more newspapers than did most other such entrepreneurs, various major magazines, and radio and television stations. In 1971 the S. I. Newhouse School of Public Communications replaced the School of Journalism. The latter's curriculum and faculty served as the core of the new institution.
3. Spencer's name always appears on lists of pioneers in American journalism education. Beside his are those of Harry F. Harrington (Northwestern University); Walter Williams (University of Missouri), who like Spencer became his university's president though Williams lacked the bachelor's degree; Frank Luther Mott (University of Iowa and University of Missouri), Pulitzer prize winning historian of journalism; and Talcott Williams (Columbia University).

ism. It brought him national recognition and many awards, as did his textbooks, three of which he wrote with me. Also on the staff were Laurance Seigfried (he was fussy about the spelling of his name), and George L. Bird, who played a key role in the development of a religion journalism curriculum.

Creation of a magazine department

When I joined these and others in the school, newspaper and magazine editorial operations were in a single department. I was asked to be the head of it. But in addition to the fact that newspapers and magazines are different disciplines, it seemed to me that a university located in the northeastern states where there were no accredited programs in magazine, should be giving that industry more prominence.

The result was that the editorial department was split. I headed the magazine department for the next 23 years. Others took over newspaper. Courses we added were magazine production, a research seminar, critical writing, a separate course for editing, an advanced course in article writing, and a specialized magazine course dealing with such areas as labor, religion, business and trade, science, and sports.

Any educator forming such a new or emerging program must think of many considerations. The questions might run like this: Which other universities in the nation offer this specialty? Which particularly in one's own area of the country? What is in the other programs? Is location an important factor? What employment opportunities exist for graduates? What cooperation can be expected from the industry itself? If a program is to be offered on a departmental basis, should there be a richer sequence justifying both an undergraduate and a graduate program?

I found myself in a department that coincided with my own writing specialties: magazine articles, critical writing, and book writing. The first two were my core courses, but later I added history of journalism, foreign press, the black press, and, finally, religion journalism, offered less regularly than the cores.[4]

Cooperation came from New York, Philadelphia, and Bos-

---

4. These added courses, for the most part, embraced both newspaper and magazine print media and were not considered as part of any one departmental core.

ton magazine offices, the Magazine Publishers Association, and the American Business Press; they provided summer internships and job offers; a few publishers sent representatives to interview seniors and graduating master's candidates.

Much later, when a doctor of philosophy program was developed for the entire school, magazine students were admitted to it and some valuable dissertations resulted. Articles based on some of these were published in *Journalism Quarterly*.

By the mid-1970s the graduate division accepted no more than two or three Ph.D. candidates a year because of an overabundance of applicants and insufficient numbers of faculty equipped to advise them. This was true even though for many years Syracuse has had one of the largest communications staffs and student bodies in the nation.

Enter Frank Laubach

The idea for religion journalism at Syracuse was planted one spring day in 1947 when I had been on the faculty only eight months. The journalism school's main office door was opened, and a tall, rangy man of about 50 approached Irene Chermak, Dean Spencer's secretary.

"I'd like to see Dean Spencer," he said.

"May I have your name?"

The stranger replied, "Frank Laubach." There had been no request for an appointment from a Mr. Laubach. The name meant nothing to Mrs. Chermak, but she went to the dean's office. Dean Spencer also had not heard of anyone named Frank Laubach. But he had Mrs. Chermak usher him in and they were soon talking in earnest.

Laubach explained himself briefly. He had just as informally visited Northwestern and Ohio State universities, he said. His mission had been to ask them to consider launching a program to train young people for service overseas as writers, editors, graphic artists, printers, and other types of skilled communicators to provide reading material for new literates. Both institutions had turned down his idea. Was Syracuse interested?

The dean asked questions before replying.

First, he wanted more information about Frank Laubach. I do not know, of course, what Dr. Laubach said. He was a modest man and probably said the minimum. He was a Congregational church pastor and missionary. And, as many persons now know from the four biographies published about Dr. Laubach and from the more than twoscore books he wrote, he first dealt with adult literacy problems in 1929 in the Philippines.

His principle was to take persons newly literate and encourage them to teach others the rudiments of reading. The slogan "Each One Teach One" grew from this procedure. The plan, begun in 1930, had spread until 1970, the year of Dr. Laubach's death, to more than 100 nations and was adapted to over 300 languages and dialects. It still is widely used.

Although the journalism administrators of three of the USA's largest secular universities were uninformed about Frank Laubach, he already was known widely on the international scene. The appreciation of his work then, however, was restrict-

Frank Laubach, the "apostle to the illiterates," inspired Syracuse University to launch a literacy journalism program in 1949. His slogan "Each One Teach One" grew from his method of encouraging a newly literate person to teach others the rudiments of reading.

ed largely to the religious world. In less than a decade his fame spread to secular society through articles in such publications as *Reader's Digest*, the *New Yorker*, and the *Atlantic Monthly*.

Frank Laubach undoubtedly confined his words to Dean Spencer that day to the problems of teaching people how to overcome their illiteracy and of providing them with suitable reading matter. As literacy workers everywhere know, it is not acceptable to adult new literates to put simple, children's reading matter into their hands. They are not interested in juveniles' books and articles and poems. They want materials, especially news, written for mature persons. They also need practical writing, especially in developing countries, having to do with the digging of latrines, or the making of simple objects for daily use, such as utensils.

As Dean Spencer later reported to me, he became interested in Laubach's proposal. His church background helped him identify with the problem at once. He promised to bring the proposal before the faculty as soon as possible. Dr. Laubach was jubilant. At last he had found a sympathetic educator in a position to do something about his call for help.

And the dean kept his word.

He called upon Dr. Bird and me to act as a committee to look into the possibilities. He asked us, assuming we thought Syracuse University could help, to draw up the details of a proposed educational and training program to be presented to the faculty for adoption or rejection or refinement.

A new program is born

Dr. Bird and I examined the existing curriculum to determine what portions could be used as part of a new program. What additional courses would be needed? At what level should the work be offered? Should it be a degree program? These were the sorts of questions we raised.

We finally recommended a battery of courses leading to a master's degree in journalism, with a specialty in religion journalism.

The types of courses varied by which master's track the students might follow: newspaper, magazine, graphic arts, or some other of the half-dozen possibilities. Two new courses were suggested: religion writing and a seminar in religion journalism, both to be taught by me. Students would be asked to adapt the other, secular-oriented courses to their specialty. Their instructors would be asked to cooperate.

Thus someone in a magazine editing course could select a magazine of religion for analysis of its editing procedures. In a news writing course, when possible, assignments could deal with religion news. That is, they would relate to the organized church or to the philosophy of religion, but not exclusively, since the students were expected to know how to handle various types of news. Candidates had the option of writing a thesis or taking a comprehensive examination.

The master's degree level was selected as best able to carry this program of courses for several reasons. Most applicants were men and women in their thirties and older, with bachelor's degrees, or other master's, and sometimes seminary degrees as well. They could not be expected to remain for the Ph.D., although a few managed to do so. Some would consider the master's as a station en route to the doctorate, which might be wanted at a later date. Mainly, they wanted the advanced degree so they could qualify to teach communications. In many overseas countries, degrees such as a master's carry more prestige and power than they do in the USA. Besides that, a master's level program would help candidates justify their absence for a year from their regular duties as missionaries or publication staff members.

As we made plans, we did not forget that Dr. Laubach's interest had been in literacy journalism. Dr. Spencer, Dr. Bird, and I believed, however, that the soundest procedure was to begin with the religion field first. Out of it would grow the literacy journalism program.

Both the School of Journalism faculty and the University Senate approved the plan, and it was offered for the first time in the 1949-50 academic year. The several early students included a number who have gone on to distinguished careers in the journalism of religion and related fields.

One of these is William H. Dudde, who brought a background of service in Argentina as pastor and literacy worker. Determined to enter religion journalism, he joined the Religious News Service staff in New York on completing his degree. From there he became a public relations man for his denomination, the Lutheran Church in America. But only temporarily. He was invited to be an assistant professor at Hislop College,

Nagpur University, India, and soon after was head of the department. The Lutheran World Federation News Bureau in Geneva, Switzerland, next claimed his abilities for several years. He returned to the USA to be a publicist and editor, heading the denomination's *Resource* magazine; in 1982 he was editor and publisher of *World Encounter*, the LCA's magazine for world community, missions, and ecumenical concerns.

Another pioneer of the Syracuse program is Dr. Doris E. Hess, an executive of the Board of Global Ministries of the United Methodist Church. She had done secular newspaper work and had college credit in journalism. After her work at Syracuse for a master's degree she was sent to the Philippines by the board, the first in her denomination to be consecrated for religion journalism. She returned to Syracuse to add a Ph.D. in communications to her degrees and has since set up workshops and advised many Third World communicators on their religion publications, training plans, and workshops.

Other early students, many of them missionaries on leave for this training or using their furloughs to obtain it, came from India, Uganda, Liberia, Peru, and various other nations on most

One of the earliest students in the religion journalism program at Syracuse was Miss Irene Singh of India.

continents. They returned usually to become leaders.

The program was expanded as planned in 1951 when Robert S. Laubach, son of Dr. and Mrs. Frank C. Laubach, joined my seminar in religion journalism. He was eager to set up a seminar in literacy communications, having traveled much with his father in his campaigns to eradicate illiteracy. After an experimental semester the course was successful. A second course, in teaching literacy, was soon added. From these developed a parallel program to religion journalism called literacy journalism, which he headed, within the magazine department, until 1981. It, too, led to a master's degree and several hundred students, international as well as American, passed through.

Thus two paths were opened to students at Syracuse, and outstanding travelers eventually journeyed on each.[5]

5. Both programs were discontinued by the early 1980s. Religion journalism was dropped when enrollment fell off sharply. Mission boards could not afford to finance study by their missionaries, and publications, publicity, and other church offices could not spare staffers who wanted to improve their skills. Literacy journalism was discontinued in 1981 despite adequate enrollment; it was the victim of decisions on the part of the Newhouse administration and the faculty, both made up of relative newcomers who did not have background on the needs of new literates the world over.

2   Early Days—
Solitude and
Ocean Storms

What childhood factors helped to grow
a future writer, teacher, and religion
journalist? It's not easy to say.

My own devotion to religion journalism developed gradually, through an assortment of interests, personal experiences, and professional opportunities. Religion, writing, journalism, and the teaching of journalism converged in my life in no structured sequence.

These various elements certainly were not inherited. I was born Rolando Edgar Wolseley,[1] an only child, in New York City on March 9, 1904 to Erminie Rath and Enrique Wolseley, neither of whom took the church or religion seriously. They were more conscious of the need to do the right thing socially rather than religiously. Having a respectable address was vital. So was dressing in the mode. When going to church was the thing to do, it was done.

My mother was born a Dietrich of German-American parents. After her father's death, her mother married a Rath, also a German-American. With this heritage, she naturally preferred Lutheranism. But I never was aware that she knew about either the man whose name that denomination bears or

---

1. The *o* of Rolando has not survived except on my birth certificate. Born in Lima, Peru, my father had evidently wished his son to have a touch of South America.

about the tenets of any of its branches. She had many Christian virtues, but she did not particularly lean upon the organized church for support.

My father, whose parents came from Eastern Europe, called himself a Roman Catholic; this seemed to mean nothing to him, for he not only did nothing about it but spoke of himself as an agnostic. My father's indifference may have made my mother less religious. My mother all her life was loving and caring to me. But she was restrained by my father and my stepfather. And during the last 45 years of her life she lived mainly in Cuba and then in Florida, so we were not able to be together much. But we wrote regularly and often.

Why my mother married Enrique Wolseley I have never understood. They did not have much in common. He had a certain charm, though. He was slender with a fine head of blond hair, dressed always a bit too conspicuously, used cologne (a man 50 years ahead of his time) and carried a cane. He owned several. My favorite was a hollow one; a rapier was in it, a type now illegal. Perhaps to give him a sense of security or style, he wore gray spats. He was courtly and gentlemanly, generous with gifts and extravagant when in the money. He took my mother to the Metropolitan Opera House in midtown New York and to big parties in stylish New York restaurants, such as Bustanoby's. He was a linguist and a lover of the arts— especially music. It was he who bent me, during our few years together, toward my interest in language and languages and also in literature, art, and music.

In their travels my parents enlarged their interest in painting and sculpture as people in the Grand Tour of Europe usually did. I benefited only a little from this but enough to set the stage for a diversity of interests that exist as strongly as ever today. The effect upon my writing was not to lead me to become a critic—since I have not the slightest talents for any of the arts— but to enable me to write journalistically about them, as I did for *Etude* and other publications. Classical music has remained as a strong emotional influence upon me.

An accountant and a salesman, my father never was successful with money until he began playing the stock market. Then he went through two fortunes. To keep going in between, he pawned my mother's jewelry. He reached his profession's peak early in this century when he became general sales manager for South America of the H. J. Heinz Co., long known for its 57 varieties of pickles. But he never equaled that again. When he was flush he liked to invite music celebrities to our Riverside Drive home. Among them were Antonio Scotti, an Italian baritone and Johanna Gadski, famous as a German soprano.

In pursuit of childhood

During these years I had few friends to play with. No one read me bedtime stories, much less acquainted me with more than the usual children's literature, such as Mother Goose nursery rhymes. I found the fairy tales of the brothers Grimm for myself just as I stumbled on Andrew Lang's fairy stories and an illustrated edition of *The Thousand and One Nights*.

Toys were there but they were few and conventional— building blocks and erector sets are all that cling to memory. Had there been more of the building of toys and not so many appealing books I might have become an architect instead of an author and journalist.

An elevated train station platform gave me my first physics lesson and newspaper job. I was living in the Bronx. At 5:30 each morning I appeared on the wooden deck beside which the trains ran. My job was to take the cord-tied bundles of New York City dailies from the end car of a certain train and walk with them to the stairway at the end of the platform. After the first few days of this routine, I decided to try to save time by hanging on to the bundles by their cords, staying on the train until the end car neared the stairs. At that point I would step off with my load.

But when I did step off, down I went on top of the bundles. The breath was knocked out of me, although the papers cushioned my tumble. Forever after I have remembered that what is on a train also has the train's momentum.

Early in my life, motion pictures were of interest to me, but not in the way they were to most youngsters. In Jersey City, New Jersey, where I lived for a few years after my mother's remarriage, the Pathé Company had studios not far from the house of distant relatives where I lived. Some of us youngsters would each afternoon go to the studios to see the stars. One of them was Pearl White, who made "The Perils of Pauline" and "The Exploits of Elaine" among other popular thriller film serials, each weekly episode ending with Pearl about to be run over by a train or thrown from a bridge. Another was Warner Oland, who played Chinese parts but was not a Chinese.

As the stars drove in from Fort Lee, where the outdoor scenes were shot, their long limousines moved slowly by the studio lanes. Miss White would lean out and sprinkle a handful of dimes toward us, much as John D. Rockefeller used to do for his followers on golf courses.

My first and last motion picture appearance occurred in connection with the Pathé Company. A film was being made that required a house like the one in which I lived. I was selected to play a major part in one scene: at least it was major to me. I was to stand near a parlor window and slowly raise the shade half way. Thus my right hand became part of cinema history.

The long journey

When I reached the age of eight, my parents decided to go abroad, partly on business. My father's duties with the H. J. Heinz Company took him and his small family to South America via Germany, France, and England, going southwest to Brazil, Uruguay, Argentina, Chile, and Peru.

This journey was taken in 1912, the year the mighty transatlantic liner, the *Titanic*, hit an iceberg in the North Atlantic. The eastward crossing of the Atlantic made by the Wolseley family was in a record-breaking German steamship, the *Kaiser Wilhelm der Grosse*, and the angled recrossing from Europe to Buenos Aires, Argentina, was in a much slower British passenger vessel, the *Highland Warrior*.

The second ship I will always remember because of weeks of sunny days in the lower North Atlantic and almost the full distance of the South Atlantic. Few other children were aboard. I had the decks largely to myself, for this was no cruise ship, with decorated swimming pools astern and no promenade deck one could circle. Some mornings I'd find unexpected new passengers who had boarded off schedule while we were midocean—dozens of flying fish wiggling on the foredeck.

These ship voyages started me on a life which so far has meant nearly 40 crossings of the Atlantic and many more journeys by water on this globe. Created by this first experience was not only a future travel writer, but also someone unceasingly curious about how others live and what other countries look like and how they meet their social and political problems.

I could hardly come away from this first long voyage without being impressed deeply by a particular incident. It involved a man I saw being carried off the *Kaiser Wilhelm* on a stretcher at Bremen, Germany, our destination in Europe. During our first two days out of New York the 14,000-ton liner had to deal with a fierce North Atlantic storm, losing a half day on the crossing as a result. The wind was so violent passengers were prohibited from going on deck. Ropes were strung through the public rooms and along corridors to keep travelers from being toppled by the pitching and rocking, for that was before the day of stabilizers, which prevent or reduce the sway.

But this man, a sea traveler of many years who had been on the *Kaiser Wilhelm* before, persuaded some crewmen to tie him into a deck chair and in turn lash the chair to the bulkhead railing. He wanted to live through the storm, to endure the water dumped on him at frequent intervals as the green seas tossed the ship. But before too long, a wave leapt the outer rail and ripped the ropes that held the chair to the bulkhead. It seized him, chair and all, and carried him over the railing and into the heaving, boiling waters. But the waves also returned him, still tied to the chair, and dashed him on the deck, smashing the chair to splinters and breaking his arms and legs. I did not see this near tragedy. But my father questioned the ambulance attendants who were taking off the passenger who loved the sea too well.

Since I like at least to witness that kind of daredevilry, I wonder if that man's performance did not provide for me an early picture of what was to become central to my life—solitude, although in the case of the passenger it was with the forces of nature. It is the daredevil who works alone, as witness those who leap canyons on a motorcycle or climb the outsides of skyscrapers. The daredevil wants all the glory for himself. Writers, too, long for glory; think of their pride in bylines.

Family lost and solitude

The nine months in Europe and South America were the end of childhood family life for me. Never much to begin with, it was now lost for good, for my mother and father were separated soon after our return.[2]

Enforced loneliness, one result of being from a broken family, became a major influence on me. It was to follow me from then on. Since I began writing while I was still in preparatory school, and without close relatives, loneliness never really ceased, it simply was ameliorated. I was childless in marriage and what few relatives I had almost all were outside the USA.

Some persons think of loneliness and solitude as times of independence. In a sense they do represent such freedom, especially if the loneliness can be borne. The writer must beat it, at least those writers must who refuse to or cannot afford to surround themselves with secretaries and electronic devices to take some of the drudgery out of creative work.

Out of that first unwelcome condition of solitude grew my satisfaction with other persons through their books, articles, and writings. During the hours of steady reading at a library table or at home on the floor with my back against a chair, I lived in other worlds. Walter Scott's *Ivanhoe* and *The Heart of Midlothian* engulfed me. Such an association of minds banished boredom forever after, although not always distress or unhappiness. During those early days I estimated that at my reading speed I could expect to complete in a lifetime about 3,000 books. That discovery was discouraging when I thought of the hundreds of classics I still had not read and the fact that new books were being printed by the thousands each year.

Nonviolence and the military academy

For several years I lived with my grandmother's cousins in New Jersey. They were all Roman Catholics but they made no effort to convert me. I did not move to their faith for reasons I cannot now recall, though it was not because of any aversion to Catholicism.

I hardly understood what being a Catholic meant. My parents' casual attitude toward religion led me to the same

2. My mother later married Alfred J. Thompson, who as a mining engineer in South America's Andes mountains, had discovered vanadium, a chemical element used to harden steel. His work there is what drew attention to him from Fulton Iron Works of St. Louis. Eventually he became vice president of the company and settled with my mother in Havana, Cuba, where Fulton sold mills for sugar plantation operators.

reaction. No television or radio preachers reached me in those years because they were not on the air. My little crystal set brought in only faint sounds that came from the tubular records of the great American inventor, Thomas A. Edison. As for public religion, I heard nothing but the platitudes, the easy answers, the hellfire and damnation threats of the evangelists of my day. It was not until I was in my teens that I began to think seriously about religion.

During these years there gradually developed what became a lifelong commitment to the ideal of nonviolent resistance to evil. Gradually I began to feel that belief in nonviolence must permeate all of a person's being and views, not just in conjunction with bearing arms or opposition to war.

No single book or sermon was responsible for my reaching the conclusion that nonviolence was inseparable from Christianity and from my own just-being-formed philosophy of life. In my incessant reading then and later I came upon the lives of Jesus of Nazareth, Tolstoy, Henry David Thoreau, Mohandas K. Gandhi, and St. Francis of Assisi. But the challenge of pacifism came to me not only through the lives of these persons, but also in the social views of H. G. Wells and George Bernard Shaw, the British writers whose stories, essays, and plays were concerned with the root causes of the social evils of that period, evils persisting as the twenty-first century approaches. Later my reading was supplemented by pulpit reference in the churches I visited in Reading, Pennsylvania, where I went to high school. The logic of Christian pacifism seemed to me inescapable—a direct example of the Sermon on the Mount being applied to modern life.

Just why I responded to this thinking with such fervor I cannot trace clearly. It probably was because my parents, not being much with me in my boyhood, did nothing to turn my beliefs in the direction of the conventions of the day. Perhaps even more than today, these conventions were based upon faith in military might and in violence in personal relations, of following the doctrine of an eye for an eye. I was free, then, to allow new or different ideas to enter my mind. It may be, too, that I was attracted to the nonviolence movement because I had traveled enough to see something of the poverty and other miseries that existed in the world.

But it was through an episode during my fourteenth year

that I had my first real opportunity of sorts to put my convictions about nonviolence to the test. For some reason, my father decided to enroll me at Kyle Military Academy, an institution for boys in Irvington-on-the-Hudson, New York. How he selected this school I do not know, but it was an unfortunate choice, in my view. Being set down in a military school appalled me. My nonviolent resistance in this event got me nowhere.

I was not to be defeated, however. On the afternoon of my arrival alone by train from New York City, I was conducted to a long dormitory building, where I was shown my bed, one among dozens. A uniform was not yet ready for me, which was fine with me, so I was told to go to a certain classroom building for my first instruction. In English composition. No credentials were given to me.

When I entered the white room, with its small window, I found a dozen or so other students sprawled around the floor and on the few chairs. The instructor sat on the edge of a table. I was neither greeted nor introduced, just ignored. Current baseball lore, scores of past games, school gossip, and complaints about the food filled the hour. The class, if it could be called that, never reached any subject remotely related to the study of English. I listened closely to the food complaints.

We shuffled back to the dormitory with admonitions to unpack our belongings and put them into narrow chests of drawers beside our beds. But by that time I had a plan. I left most of my underwear, shirts, and socks in the bag and put a few larger pieces in the chest, shoving the bag under the bed, as all others had done.

A bell rang for the evening meal, at the extraordinarily early time of 4:30. We formed into lines and stood in the open air alongside bushes as tall as ourselves. Spotting a small break in them big enough for me to slip through, I left the line and walked rapidly down an incline out of sight. I went back to the dorm, grabbed my bag, and slid out the side door unnoticed and on downtown to the railway station.

I had a nervous half hour wait for a train, thinking a posse would be hunting me any minute. On reaching Grand Central Station in midtown New York, 25 miles away, I telephoned my father, who was still living alone in Manhattan. I expected a tongue lashing. Instead he said that he did not blame me and offered to come for me. I had enough money, however, to reach my New Jersey relatives. They, too, were sympathetic. Already a theoretical pacifist from my reading, I wanted nothing more to do with military academies.

Four months later I moved to Reading, Pennsylvania, where my father had enrolled me in Schuylkill Seminary. This was a combination four-year preparatory school, two-year junior college, and theological seminary run by what was then known as the Evangelical (German) denomination.[3] There for the first time the scattered exposure to church life came into some kind of focus, hazy as it was. In that Berks County city, often called Pretzel Town, the relationship between writing and religion first occurred to me. It was there that I grew to take religion seriously and in addition, to do my first work in journalism.

3. My father had selected Schuylkill, because a nephew from Lima, Peru, had attended briefly and liked it, perhaps because so many other Latin American boys were there. My father paid tuition, room, and board. Not long after that he moved to Spain, and I never saw him again.

3   Awakening to Journalism and Religion

What contributed to education and spiritual growth? Books, early newspaper work, journalists, religious thinkers, church going, seminary students, the Bible—all of these.

Set in a valley under Mt. Penn on the outskirts of Reading, Schuylkill Seminary was named for a river connected to the Delaware at Philadelphia. I shall never forget this river because I was nearly drowned in it. One summer when I was selling Fuller brushes in the Pennsylvania countryside, one of my fellow students and co-workers stood up in a canoe we were in and overturned it. Somehow, we lived long enough to reach the riverbank.

Already a bookish kid who had patronized branch libraries in four cities, I used the campus and Reading public libraries diligently. From one or the other I checked out what classics appealed to me. What riches of storytelling I discovered in Sir Walter Scott's *Rob Roy*, *Waverly*, and *Guy Mannering*. Charles Dickens provided more good stories; he attracted me because they were about the poor and the ordinary people of England and because he worked as a reporter. His *Pickwick Papers*,

Oliver Twist, and *David Copperfield* were among the many novels I liked.

From the French writers, in translation, I liked best Romain Rolland (attracted at first by his last name) for his great *Jean Christophe*. And Guy de Maupassant, for his short stories. James Fenimore Cooper, Jack London, and Mark Twain were my American favorites: for Cooper's *The Spy* and *The Last of the Mohicans*; London's *Martin Eden*, *The Call of the Wild*, and *The Sea Wolf*; and Twain's *Tom Sawyer* and *Huckleberry Finn*. In spite of the strong Spanish influence in my family, only Miguel de Cervantes, that nation's one world renowned figure as poet, playwright, and novelist, attracted me then. His most famous work, *Don Quixote*, I read several times and still am drawn to its various stage, ballet, opera, symphony, movie, and television versions.

Why was I drawn to such adventure and fantasy? My selection of these writings is easy to explain. I was alone, coming from a broken family in which, even when we were together, I had received little attention. Thus I surrounded myself with imaginary people who were sometimes more real than living persons I saw in school or other settings. These authors took me deeply into the lives of their characters, especially Dickens and Cervantes. It was as storytellers that they held me.

Their practical influence upon me directly as a future writer was slight. For a while, after I did my first newspaper work in high school, I wanted to be a novelist. I had come to believe that journalism was the royal road to literary fame. I already knew of a few successful travelers down that road— Jack London, Charles Dickens, Richard Harding Davis, Mark Twain, and, later, Ernest Hemingway.

But I had no natural storytelling ability, and my attempts at such writing stopped after a few opening pages. I did not know where to go from there, and I was unwilling to be what Robert Louis Stevenson called a "sedulous ape," that is, a writer who carefully studies the style of others in order to improve his or her own.

It was not until years later that I learned something about all the work that goes into planning a novel. And newspaper work—even school and college journalism, in the early years— I had done for too long. I was chained to facts, which is one of the reasons one should not stay on the royal road too long.[1]

But such reading of imaginative literature did affect me as a person, making of me perhaps more of a romantic, a dreamer, than I might otherwise have been. And, possibly, endowing me with respect for certain ideals, largely conventional to be sure: sympathetic to underdogs (London and Rolland), admiring of moral courage (Cervantes and Bunyan) and appreciative of humorous characters (Dickens). I read *Pilgrim's Progress* twice in those years (in my opinion few books stand that test) for about the same reason that I read Daniel Defoe: straightforwardness in construction and style, simplicity of narrative, and, in the instance of Bunyan, an interest in the theological aspects, some of which in time I found unconvincing.

A reporter at large

While at Schuylkill I wrote for the *Schuylkill News*, the student newspaper, but was more interested in the *Narrator*, the literary magazine on which I was successively news editor, assistant editor, and associate editor. During afternoons, holidays, and summer vacations I worked on one or the other of three of the four local Reading, Pennsylvania, dailies.[2] I also was an out-of-town correspondent for the venerable Philadelphia *North American*. One of my best school friends, Elmer Miller, also worked for the Reading papers. We used to go down to the offices together until one day his paper ruled that he must not be seen with me in town for fear we would betray stories to each other.

Like every other neophyte reporter, I at first had anything but choice assignments. Hospital, obituary, and boys club news were my beat. I was a stringer, paid by my weekly string. That is, my clippings were pasted end-to-end as a measure of the

1. Perhaps another factor that dampened my novelist ambitions was that in those days, especially in some religious circles, the writing and reading of novels was considered sinful and a waste of time. Unlike poetry and plays, novels had few illustrious figures to give them respectability: their authors were not Shakespeare or Wordsworth, not Milton or Coleridge. One of them was the so-called evil-minded Thomas Hardy; another was Theodore Dreiser.
2. The papers were the Reading *Herald-Telegram*, *News-Times*, *Tribune*, and *Eagle*. The publication of four competing dailies in that small city points up the enormous change that has taken place in USA journalism in the past half century. Today not even New York or any other large city has more than two or three competing general newspapers and even where there are two often they are owned by the same firm. New York in the 1920s had seven.

space I had filled. They brought me five cents an inch or a dollar a column. When I began exceeding the salary of full-time reporters I was put down for $15 a week regularly, an average wage in those days for cubs.

The reporter's job today can no more be compared with that of the 1920s and 1930s than the work of a telephone operator, a typist, or a typesetter. Much writing then was being done by hand, to the distress of those in the back shop who had to decipher it. The enormous public relations profession, with its tools of publicity and promotion, had relatively little place. And the present-day computerized newsrooms were not even dreamed of by some Jules Verne of journalism.

Reporting was a relatively simple procedure then. A city editor left a list of assignments on his desk for the day's or next day's paper. As reporters checked in they studied the assignment book or pad for their names and any special orders. The newsmen—and then they were mainly men—then set about covering their stories—telephoning, consulting files, and interviewing sources, thus obtaining the needed facts in each assignment. Or they rushed to the scene of an accident or fire or some other calamity. Facts in, they then drafted their stories by hand or created first drafts directly on a typewriter, turned the sheets in to the desk, and did other jobs as needed: perhaps desk work, advance preparations for stories they knew were coming up the next day, checking proofs of their own material, even seeing their copy through in hard metal in the page form from which a plate was to be made for use on a press. Electronics, word processors, and computers today have taken over many of these operations.

But even with conditions the way they were in the 1920s, I found the work exciting. I enjoyed learning the news before the general public did. It attracted me to a journalism career, as it did my friend Elmer Miller, who became editor in chief and vice president of a substantial daily in eastern New York State.

A taste of religion news

The religion news I gathered was largely routine, obtained partly over the telephone and partly on foot at nearby buildings. Few churches sent in news of their own accord; pastors or secretaries rarely recognized a news story when they saw one or understood news policies and values. Instead, they scolded the press for printing what they called only bad news. They failed to realize that so long as bad news is the exception, the general situation is sound, and the day only good news is the news, the situation is unsound basically. Those clergy who submitted material, usually hand-delivered by the preacher, often turned in badly written copy in need of following up. For example, the original writer would omit full names or forget important dates and locations of forthcoming events.

This experience, however, was to give me an interest in church and religion news that later would be developed. I became closely acquainted with the special pages of newspapers and with denominational and other religion magazines. Such interest led to my involvement in the Syracuse religion journalism program and eventually to my producing books, university courses, and training programs for religion journalists and writers for periodicals of religion and the organized church.

But in these early days, I did not see the importance of religion news nor realize how miserable was the coverage of it by most general papers. There it was considered unimportant unless it brought in substantial amounts of advertising revenue, as at Christmas and Easter.

I did have a taste of this, however. The city editor of one paper I worked for in Reading was a local pastor. He had a small charge nearby in the country. If ever there was a misfit in the pulpit as well as in the city room this man was. Stocky, dressed like one of the city's bums, always sweaty, a live and cheap cigar stuck in his mouth even when he talked, which he did in a petulant, grating voice, he was foul-mouthed and blasphemous.

That was bad enough. Despite his church connection, he printed only those notices that were from churches that advertised in the paper. Thus the church page each Saturday was a swamp of paid and unpaid notices of sermon topics and other Sunday church news, crowding out more important religion or church information. His fat torso twisting and bobbing as he raged at the staff, he was dictatorial and without hesitation took revenge upon those who challenged his practices. He ran the rather shabby newsroom as if it were a military unit.

All this has changed, now, at least among the best papers in the USA. Significant news of religion and long analytical stories of trends and developments in the world of religion are common in leading dailies. While there still is too much of it, routine news has changed as well. And what is only routine sometimes gives way to firsthand coverage by full-time staffers who know something about theology, church history, and the current tensions and problems of the denominations and other religious institutions. Some of the best writing and photography in the newspapers appears on the church and religion pages of those elitist publications. I base this strong assertion on my service as a judge of contests for the Religion Newswriters Association and of state newspaper associations, and my exposure to various newspapers as a matter of professional habit.

Religion around me

During my five years of studying and writing news stories in Reading, I gained impressions of the world of religion not easy to forget. My exposure was too limited to be a scientific survey, but subsequent events show that it was sound for the time. One source of my evidence was the conduct of certain of the School of Theology students. All were men, of course, for it was long before the time when women would be welcome in such schools.

Properly pious all week, on Saturday nights a dozen or so exhibited what then were their desires. There probably were tensions that caused them to do what they did, contradictory as it was with their public professions. Some would return about midnight from fun on the town, as they thought of it, too tipsy to find their dormitory rooms without help. Others stayed away all night, having gone to Philadelphia to visit the girls in the red-light district. These returned to campus by early morning buses or trains, snatched a little sleep and breakfast, and then went to their country charges, using as sermons papers prepared in homiletics classes.

For a long time I was cynical about these seminary students until I came to know more of them elsewhere and to see that this was a minority. Some of these young men disappeared from the pastoral ranks after a time and at least a few others straightened out and had useful careers.

Between these divinity students and the obnoxious pastor playing at hard-boiled city editor, I gained a low impression of churchmen. It was unfair, however, for most of the young Schuylkill would-be preachers were diligent, honest, and sincere. And the city editor, too, was an exception. The other such functionaries in Reading and elsewhere I subsequently worked for were of a different stripe: efficient and generally kind.

My own church going, while not discriminating enough perhaps, was at least varied and gave me broad exposure to preaching, doctrine, and church operations. The denominational range was wide, from Evangelical (Church of Germany), Presbyterian, and Friends, to Universalist. Reading was considered a religiously strong area. Pennsylvania, in general, has noted and unusual church connections, such as the Amish and Mennonites. Major preachers visited the city, under auspices of the School of Theology. One such was Reinhold Niebuhr, not then as prominent a Protestant preacher and theologian as he became. I soon forgot the ideas he offered in the old wooden chapel at the seminary. But years later, when reading his significant book *Moral Man and Immoral Society* and encountering basic differences in our views, there were echoes of them from the past.[3]

My reaction to the church sermons I attended, as distinguished from those heard in the seminary chapel, varied according to the church. I found, as I still do, the evangelical and fundamentalist services undisciplined and insufficiently reverential. Being in a school with compulsory chapel, I had an overdose of services that blended worship with social time. On the other hand, I found that the Episcopalians went to the other extreme of too much formality. Also in the denominational churches the socializing in the narthex annoyed me but not as much as did the whispering, the gossiping, and, above all, the Sunday-only religion of some members.

That was why I not only went to mainline churches, but also to the Quakers and to the offbeat ones such as Universalist. The two less popular groups impressed me as generally sincere and willing to apply their doctrines beyond the personal life to society as a whole.

It was a long time before I had any clear understanding of the place of prayer in church and personal life. I found after

---

3. These fundamental differences were over man's ability, as I thought of it, to live Christ's ideals in defiance of man's laws, especially as applied to the problem of war and peace and to the use of violence in labor relations. I still have the 1932 edition of Niebuhr's book and read again with even greater disbelief his assertion that "nonviolence does coerce and destroy." Then there is the confusion of terms in which Niebuhr wrapped his argument as well as the acceptance of the belief that nonviolence is, in his words, "a morally impossible instrument of social change."

joining the denomination to which I still belong, the United Methodist, that I tried to be a faithful worshiper of Jesus, by which I do not mean that I was a successful one. I failed, as I still do, at many points, since, for example, I still must push myself to love my enemies and not rejoice in the afflictions that befall them.

Kennedy, Holmes, Fosdick

There were other religious leaders who came to Reading. One was A. Studdart Kennedy, ruddy, stocky, and hearty, typically British in accent and manner. From New York City were John Haynes Holmes and Harry Emerson Fosdick, both filled with unconventional social ideas for the time and both intellectually exciting and challenging. All three moved me deeply, presenting a more humane outlook and philosophy than did Niebuhr, who was the pragmatist first and then the humanist. Their social ideas, though controversial, attracted me because they were so unlike the accepting views of society I heard in school and in most town religious ceremonies.

The formation of my religious views came partly from them and partly from others, most now forgotten. Holmes's literary versatility was what first attracted me. He was a close student and analyst of Walter Scott's poetry, and he also was a playwright. But his opposition to capital punishment and racism, his championship of civil rights and what he called the revolutionary function of the organized church, plus his puncturing of bombastic, flag-waving patriotism impressed me the most. All these causes seemed to me thereafter the proper sphere of Christians and their institutions.

Harry Emerson Fosdick I heard before he was chief minister of Riverside Church in New York. Through him I became interested in Rufus Jones, leading to occasional attendance at the Quaker meeting in Reading. Fosdick was a Baptist and his theology more orthodox than that of the Unitarian Holmes, but none the less courageous when it came to applying the Gospel to social issues.

Perhaps from the influence of these preachers, the life principles that arise from my religious beliefs do not exist in an iron box or frame, never to be altered or modified by the test of reality, my own meditations, or the thinking and writing of others. This position may be considered slackness of character or treason of doctrine. That may be so, but only a closed mind can go through life without ever questioning the rules, wherever they exist or from whatever source. God did not put people on earth to be mere automatons. Blind, unthinking acceptance should not be expected of God's free agents.

Reading the Bible

My reading about religion as a philosophy at this time, the early 1920s, was minor. I bought in 1920 my first copy of the Bible, an 1895 edition of a Holman. I wish I could record that I drew constantly upon all of the Bible for both spiritual nurture and style, as so many far-better-known writers than I say they did. But I read it selectively. I felt that to read it in a marathon, as do some worshipers of the Bible, is to debase rather than appreciate it.

In another copy of the Bible, its date of acquisition not noted but in the family since 1940, I have kept a clipping I had cut from a church bulletin somewhere. It speaks for me. It is a hymn by George Croly:

> Spirit of God, descend upon my heart;
> Wean it from earth; through all its pulses move;
> Stoop to my weakness, mighty as Thou art,
> And make me love Thee as I ought to love.
>
> Teach me to feel that Thou art always nigh;
> Teach me the struggles of the soul to bear;
> To check the rising doubt, the rebel sigh;
> Teach me the patience of unanswered prayer.

Yet it speaks for me only in part. There is one line I do not accept or perhaps misunderstand: "Teach me . . . to check the rebel sigh." Jesus was a rebel.

So superficial and cloying was much of the religious activity on campus that I was glad to be out of it, when graduation came, on that score if no other. I revolted against the stream of religious jargon fired at the students, laced with authoritarianism. Instead I read the religious and literary classics devotedly, especially Nathaniel Hawthorne from Massachusetts and Rabindranath Tagore of India. The only title of Tagore that sticks in memory was his book of poems, *Gitanjali*.

But from that and reading about him I realized I had come upon a man of peace who not only opposed violence but also national pride, so often the cause of wars.

Readings in journalism

Practical books relating to journalism that I read during this time were gifts from my mother. They nurtured my interest in writing, especially a career in journalism. A few still are in my library, more than half a century later.

The first and one of the most absorbing to me was Philip Gibbs's *Adventures in Journalism.* An English foreign and war correspondent and popular novelist, he was knighted for his work, which appeared in leading British and USA newspapers. Part of the attraction for me was that he was a professional editorial worker at 19, therefore giving me hope.[4]

This book and others by Gibbs made foreign correspondence appear to be a glamorous career. Writers are able to travel and be paid to do it. Yet Sir Philip's book and others by his colleagues in journalism never moved me to try for an appointment in the field. I had a taste of it while I lived in India, much later on, by writing free lance for U.S. newspapers and magazines. I can explain why I did not do more only by saying I lacked the proper adventurous spirit and a reluctance, after I was married, to be separated for long periods from my wife.

When my mother went to a large Fifth Avenue store to buy another book for me she had trouble finding it. It was *The Story of the Sun* by Edward J. O'Brien, once editor of that famous New York daily.[5] When she asked for it in one section, the clerk sent her to another: astronomy. The second clerk could not find it either. By then my mother realized what was happening. She explained that the sun she meant was a newspaper, not an inhabitant of the sky. It was found under history.

Reading O'Brien's account of the *Sun* headed me toward

---

4. In 1962, when he died at the age of 84, the usually careful *New York Times* recorded his date of birth as 1777. Since he was a *Times* writer during his great career this flub seemed to me especially ludicrous.
5. The *Sun*, known to the public for printing the editorial "Yes, Virginia, there is a Santa Claus," was one of the first papers in the USA to be known as "penny papers," because of their price. It became famous under its dynamo of an editor, Charles Anderson Dana. But it is remembered also for the moon hoax story it carried in 1835, written by Richard Adams Locke. That bit of fakery trebled its circulation. He described life on the moon, portraying batmen as inhabiters.

books on its rivals and their editors. One of these was James Gordon Bennett, who, in the *New York Morning Herald*, injected new energy into the press, pepping up even its religion news, sensationalizing many news stories, and inventing the interview technique. Another was Horace Greeley, who in 1841 founded a penny sheet for New York City—the *Tribune*. It survives to this day in the name of the *International Herald Tribune* read by travelers in many parts of the world.

These editors nurtured my desire for a chance at newspaper work myself, and motivated me to do the work as stringer for the Philadelphia *North American*, also a great daily in its day. The books and the actual work wiped away whatever slight interest I had in any other occupation. With both journalism and the journalism teaching that followed, I never wavered in reaching the vocational goal I had picked.

4

On to Northwestern

Certain teachers were a key influence on the student journalist—Baker Brownell, Lawrence Martin, Ernest Lauer, Kenneth Colegrove. There was also a Methodist pastor, Ernest Fremont Tittle.

The educational process, formal or informal, perhaps is the best example we have of perpetual motion, only it is mental instead of physical. Five years of it at Schuylkill had to affect me. I certainly was no genius as far as memory was concerned. I could scarcely memorize a six-line poem and even now must rehearse for a long time to remember anything not used constantly in daily life. Mathematics and science baffled me; English delighted me, as did study of Spanish and German, history and civics.

Journalism students, ever since that study was begun more than a half century ago, are likely to respond to formal, early education the way I did. They are naturally curious and tend to resent the inflexibility of the more rigid studies. Through years of examining high school and college records of university applicants for journalism education, advising such students at the various institutions where I have taught, and seeing their performance, this affinity for the so-called less exact subjects is obvious. Especially is this true among the students of writing and editing. Exceptions are the few who become science or technical writers or editors.

My lack of sympathy for the natural sciences and mathematics went logically with my preference for imaginative literature. It may, on the other hand, seem like a contradiction for me at the same time to have been so enthusiastic about journalism. That work, presumably, is dedicated to reporting the truth, to reaching total accuracy as nearly as it can be attained, to caring about exact details. And indeed it is a contradiction if one thinks of journalists as robots diligently producing foolproof copy. Journalism, however, like all disciplines, is creative as well as exact. And it is in conceiving a news story—for example, seeing it in the mind's eye whole, from only the fragments of information in a notebook—that the journalist is an artist. The sculptor knows what to remove from the clay; the writer must know what facts to use and what not.

Move to Medill

My devotion went largely to what journalism it was possible to practice in Reading. Then, when I was 16, at the suggestion of Professor Roger Kratz, one of my favorite teachers partly because he took a personal interest in my future, I began looking about for schools of journalism. Professor Kratz suggested his alma mater and let me borrow its yearbook. After seeing it I was determined to attend Northwestern's Medill School of Journalism in Evanston, Illinois. That determination became a reality in the fall of 1923.

But desire for experience in university journalism soon put me in trouble on the Northwestern campus. During registration, a table outside one of the buildings held a sign that read: "Sign up here for the *Daily Northwestern* staff." I wrote my name unhesitatingly on the sheet below the sign.

The next day the signers were called together and given assignments. Mine was to assemble certain enrollment facts from all administrative offices of the constituent colleges. I was told to visit each. Registration days in college business offices are bedlam, with long lines and everyone under pressure. After several failures to penetrate offices or obtain cooperation once in, I returned to the assignment room.

"Wouldn't it be a better idea to telephone these offices instead of trying to fight the lines to get this simple information?" I suggested to the tall young editor on duty.

"No."

"But that's the way such stories are covered where I worked on several daily papers in Reading, Pennsylvania."

The editor bridled. "Well, well. So that's the way it was done in Reading, Pee-A, huh? How good of you to share your great experience with us. But that's not our way of doing things. Now get yourself out of here and go to those offices, if you want to work for this paper."

I tossed the assignment sheet on his desk and walked off. That first semester I did not work for the *Daily Northwestern*. But over the next three and a half years I eventually wrote many stories and started a regular literary column of book news and reviews, a job to be important to my career in journalism.

Teachers of influence

Such college boy writing and reporting was by no means all I derived from my time at Northwestern as an undergraduate. During the four years, I was enrolled in standard courses in the Medill School of Journalism, established with aid from the *Chicago Tribune* and therefore named for Joseph Medill, the newspaper's founder.

My most stimulating teachers at Medill were Baker Brownell, the modest philosopher, and Lawrence Martin, who taught article writing and far transcended the journeyman journalist types who dominated most schools. Brownell, a serious but not humorless teacher, in his time affected the lives of more Medill students than anyone before him. Although he was a professor of journalism, having been an editorial writer for several Chicago dailies, he held a chair in philosophy at Northwestern as well. His was a questioning and original mind that moved me ever to challenge everyday assumptions about politics, the arts, and particularly, journalism.

Brownell's major course was "Contemporary Affairs," and the largest room in the building always was crowded. He now and then introduced us to some of the nation's leading thinkers, such as Max Otto, the University of Wisconsin's outstanding philosopher, or leading nonthinkers, such as the

Chicago Tribune's editor and publisher Colonel Robert R. McCormick. He demanded that we keep a running diary of our reading, reaction to his and the visiting lecturers' presentations, and analysis of the class discussions. This was excellent preparation for writing theses and books.[1]

Lawrence Martin was one of the Northwestern teachers who influenced me not only with his writing methods, attitudes toward journalism, and social ideals, but also with his teaching techniques. This impact he shared with Brownell. Martin was temperamentally different from Brownell but, like him, was an original thinker and stylist. He was the kind of teacher who is not content to tell and show his students how to write what he is teaching them to write but insists on doing it himself in the professional field.

Thus, while on the Medill faculty, he was writing frequently for *Esquire* and the now forgotten intellectual monthly *Coronet* as well as lesser magazines. One experience he enjoyed relating to us was how he first broke into *Esquire*. He had submitted an article, which was rejected promptly. He gave it to a smaller Chicago periodical. Not long after, he attended a banquet and sat next to Arnold Gingrich, the noted American magazine editor who was the heart and soul of the original *Esquire*.

"Saw your article in (I have forgotten what magazine Martin had given it to) and liked it," Gingrich said.

Martin thanked him.

"Why didn't you send that to us? It's just the sort of thing we like."

Martin explained. Gingrich asked to have it. Martin obtained permission from the smaller publication, a nonpaying college periodical, and made a substantial sale. Many lessons for writers come from this incident: aim high at first, keep trying with national magazines, do not be discouraged too easily, and come to know editors personally.

Eventually Martin resigned his teaching post and joined Esquire, Inc., as an editor. After marrying one of his students, also a gifted writer, he turned to travel writing and with her or alone turned out a half-dozen books and innumerable articles.

---

1. Brownell himself wrote seminal books, such as *Earth Is Enough, Architecture and Modern Life* (with Frank Lloyd Wright), *The New Universe, Art Is Action*, and *The Human Community*.

He added foreign correspondence to his production at the same time, encouraging foreign correspondents to take advantage of being in foreign countries to write for travel magazines and sections.

Because I knew Martin well enough to be behind the scenes of his writing methods, I recalled them in the early 1970s when I began to do travel journalism more seriously than I had earlier. And I have continued to profit by imitating the Martin mode. He was more concerned than any of his competitors with originality and briskness of style, he was free of the promotional hoopla found so often in books for tourists, he was interested in the history of the places he wrote about, and he remembered the practical problems travelers face.

Outside the journalism school faculty were other teachers who influenced me. Notable were Ernest Lauer, who taught U.S. history, and Kenneth Colegrove, a political scientist. Two more opposite personalities cannot be imagined. Lauer, a quiet man who suffered from amnesia, was warm and sympathetic to students with problems. As a social and political liberal, he helped nurture in me what social conscience had been planted earlier by three Schuylkill teachers—the brothers Wentzel. Fred Wentzel, especially, had touched me with his poetry and his religiously based social passion more than he did with his Latin instruction. His brothers, Jake, who taught German, and Bill, whose courses were in the sciences, were both flamboyant, by comparison, and less high-minded, and Jake was trenchantly skeptical about conventional religion.

Colegrove, in contrast to Lauer, was stern, a thin man with a narrow face, who seemed cold and uninterested in his students. He was as rigid in his political thinking as he was in his posture. I appreciated his scrupulous scholarship, his insistence that his students check and double-check all statements of fact, that footnotes be faultless, and that sources be completely stated. Such rules were excellent for journalism students. It certainly set a standard for me in my work. And it was passed along to all my students thereafter.

Newspaper work in Chicago and Evanston
The professional newspaper work I did in Chicago and Evanston during these years at Northwestern kept alive as much as did my journalism classes the plan to be a writer. Chicago

then had five dailies. One, the *Chicago Evening Post*, attempted to emulate the old *New York Evening Post* of the days when William Cullen Bryant, the poet ("Thanatopsis" and "To a Waterfowl"), was its editor.[2] The Chicago paper ran sober editorials and serious columns on public affairs and, exceptional for its time, complete texts of important public speeches, reports, and sermons. Considerable original foreign correspondence appeared as well.

One of the two supplements it offered its readers was important to me: a Thursday art section and on Fridays a *Literary Review* like the tabloid book review and literary articles that appear in special inserts in the *Christian Science Monitor* and the *New York Times*.

The *Friday Literary Review* was edited by Llewellyn Jones, a chubby, ruddy Welshman with sandy red hair, a gifted critic, one of the few in the Midwest at that time recognized by the snobbish literary elite of the East who thought the literary United States ended at Albany, New York. I liked his book section and especially his great interest in the Danish pastor, poet, historian, and educator, N.F.S. Grundtvig, about whom he eventually became an authority, publishing a book on him. Grundtvig interested me because he was a reformer, challenging the accepted views of Christianity of his day, and also founder of the folk school plan now strong throughout Scandinavia.

I walked into the *Post* building one afternoon and sought Mr. Jones. I found him at a desk the top of which was mostly book piles. I introduced myself, showing him copies of my literary column in the *Northwestern*. After I finished he said nothing. Instead, he swiveled in his chair and pointed to a four-tier bookcase filled with colorfully jacketed review copies sent free by publishers.

"Take one or two," he said, "and try your hand."

Then he gave me several sheets with brief instructions on how to write book reviews and criticisms. This assignment was the first of many I was to have from him. Soon my byline appeared in the *FLR*. My education was being kept moving faster than ever now.

---

2. Few journalists know that Bryant was the *Post's* chief editor for 49 years; he made it a dignified and substantial daily.

Tennis and a first check

Not only did I work with newspapers, but I also launched another career that was to occupy much of my time as a journalist for the rest of my life. I did my first free-lance writing for magazines in my freshman year with an article for a sports magazine published by Bernarr Macfadden, the physical culturist and successful entrepreneur with mass magazines, including *Physical Culture* and *True Story*. The piece for *Sportlife* was a true story indeed, for it was about the young tennis players of the United States.

I had gathered my material while working as a court marker and roller early in the mornings of a week-long national tournament some miles from campus. Being a tennis player myself, I was able to discuss details with the younger players. I came to know many of these promising players, some later to be stars, as well as world-famous court figures of the day: William T. Tilden, still considered by some to be the greatest player of all time; Helen Wills, a woman's champion; Babe Norton, the clown of the courts, and Bill Johnston, second only to Tilden.

When the tournament was over, I wrote the article and submitted it without querying the editor. I was such a neophyte it never occurred to me to ask these youths for photographs; the editor supplied them.

My first check for this type of writing amounted to all of $30, really not a bad fee in those days. So proud of it was I that I pinned it to a black coat and took a picture of it. Unfortunately I was not much of a photographer, for all that resulted was a picture of a white rectangle. Blank.

Challenges to journalism education

Meanwhile my journalism training and general education continued on the Northwestern campus. Education for journalism then was much in need of defense. Medill was one of the more respected schools and not so much the butt of attacks from uninformed editors and publishers who never had even visited the buildings of such outstanding schools as Columbia, Missouri, and Iowa.

The challenges to communications education that continue sometimes are deserved by certain schools and departments but not by the majority. The complaints go further than saying that graduates cannot spell correctly or write clear sentences. One adverse criticism heard from some editors and publishers is that the students are given too much exposure to theory rather than practice, or enrolled in classes such as the social sciences that are seemingly of no immediate use to them.

Another criticism is that schools of journalism, not to mention the journalism industry, lack social and ethical vision. Teachers of communications in the USA, as a rule, usually have upheld the idea that the press and other media should try at least to approximate objectivity. Journalists face the problem daily, even though they admit that complete objectivity is unreachable as an absolute. One more explanation might be the absence of religiously motivated persons in the faculties of the schools and on the staffs of the publications or stations. I am not saying that there are none, but they are few. Not as proof, but as an example of an attitude, I want to relate this experience.

I was in the office of a senior editor of *Time*, now a member of the upper echelon of Time, Inc., one of the major corporations in the communications business. We were talking about his duties when the mail was brought to his desk. He began to sort it. He picked up *Christian Century*, an independent liberal Protestant weekly magazine, which is delivered without a wrapper. In a second he tossed it into the waste basket, not even glancing to see the titles of the articles in it. People in communications are often so busy or indifferent that they simply are uninformed about religion. They also lack association with great religious leaders.

Tittle, a man ahead of his time

This is one reason why I treasure my opportunity as a young man to come to know well one of the great religious leaders of his time: Ernest Fremont Tittle, pastor of the First Methodist Church of Evanston.[3] During 24 years of his pastorate, I was in his congregation, serving on the official board, on the Commission on World Peace and other committees, and aiding in that large church's publishing and publicity work.

During those same years my first wife, Bernice, was Dr.

---

3. The church is now known as the First United Methodist Church and is often considered the "Cathedral of Methodism." See Robert Moats Miller's biography, *How Shall They Hear Without a Preacher?: The Life of Ernest Fremont Tittle*. Chapel Hill: University of North Carolina Press, 1971.

Tittle's personal secretary and for over two thirds of those years, manager of the large church office, at times with a staff of seven. It was through her that I became a member of the church and the denomination. Bernice and I came to know Ernest and Glenna Tittle well, at times occupying the parsonage when they were away.

Already exposed to Lutheranism, Unitarianism, and the services now and then of churches of other denominations, I responded eagerly to the views of Ernest Tittle. His ideas took seed quickly through his sermons, books, and personal counseling. He stood for much that I already accepted and much that I had started to champion during the years when he was my moral and religious mentor. He was a man far ahead of his time.

Today the world can see the rightness of his views on racial justice, war and peace, and economic equity. Certain of those views I had learned from others before him, not only Mohandas Gandhi, George Bernard Shaw, and H. G. Wells, whom I have already mentioned, but also Henry David Thoreau (*Walden* and *Civil Disobedience*). There also was in the religious world irregular reading in the works of the three famous Thomases: à Becket, à Kempis, and Aquinas. Ernest Tittle kept them alive and made new applications for me.

As a human being my pastor was not easily forgotten. He was thought of as a man's man: an outdoorsman, rugged in appearance, forceful of handshake. He had a firm, almost bulldog jaw. His broad shoulders made him look brawnier than he really was, but inside he was highly sensitive.

Though he was a serious thinker, he tried in his sermons and lectures to avoid the church jargon that plagues so many speakers from pulpits and lecterns. No one ever complained that he was obscure, trite, or technical in his language. Some members of his congregation, on the contrary, did not fully appreciate his efforts at being clear and holding or gaining attention.

Betsy Tittle Poston, his only daughter, recalls that on several occasions her father would start a Bible quotation by saying, "Once upon a time . . ." or "There's a story in the Bible about . . ."

"Invariably," Mrs. Poston says, "a few members of the congregation would become irate—and at least one person left the church because of these 'irreverent' remarks."

Of special interest to me was Ernest Tittle's writing. He was a capable and painstaking craftsman, tireless about finding the right word for what he had to say. He worried about his grammar, his word choice, his use of writing techniques, and the organization of his manuscripts. He revised and then revised again. When he went into the pulpit he had a few notes before him, but he had worked out all details beforehand. He welcomed criticism of his writing and never hesitated to consult close associates about the technical problems he was encountering as a writer. His dozen books show the results of such meticulous work, especially since he had to change most of what he had written, which was for the ear, into material for the eye to scan.

He was influential in my life for another reason. Though he was a controversial preacher, he loved and was concerned about the individual member of his congregation. For this reason, when the political extremists attacked his claim to a free pulpit, even the most conservative official board member defended his right to free expression. The First Church parishioners loved him because he loved them.

I learned from Ernest Tittle that one can say much in the spirit of love that others would say with hate in their voices and be hated in return. When I myself have been subject to public attack, I have tried to remember Ernest Tittle and turned away wrath as well as I could by attempting, as he did, to be patient with and understanding of opponents.

One test of this occurred in India, while I was teaching as a Fulbright professor in the early 1950s. I was expected, having State Department support for the assignment, to speak in behalf of my own country before various groups. At many meetings, almost the first question following my presentation, asked in an accusatory voice, was why the USA discriminates against its minorities, especially people of black skin. At times the question was not one at all, but an accusation, couched in sarcastic, abusive language. My reply was what I thought Ernest Tittle would give under the same circumstances.

Thus the impact of his life on me was personal, but it also had a professional effect. He also influenced me to lend more of my journalism training and experience to the service of the church. It was carried out—and has not yet ended—for many years as a small return for the education I received from an important church with a pioneering pastor at its head. As it turned out, the perpetual motion of education was to be strongest in the world of religion.

5 Railroad PR Man, City Editor, Faculty Member

The writer and a question of ethics.
Publicizing the church.
Teachers, writing, and students.
A pacifist at Northwestern—conviction
under pressure.

After graduation from Northwestern in 1928 when jobs were hard to find, I at last landed one in the public relations department of the Pennsylvania Railroad. The company had large offices in Union Station in downtown Chicago. For three years I worked there, helping write and edit its biweekly regional tabloid, one of three that covered the system, with a circulation of more than 300,000. One of those years I was managing editor, but it was just a paper designation, for on the line's payroll all but the editor were listed as clerks. This well-run paper was, in fact, the house organ for the company.

This job led me to my first important professional ethical problem in news work. Someone had written about the glories of life in house organ journalism. The article appeared in the *Quill*, the monthly of what now is called The Society for Journalists, Sigma Delta Chi. The author could find no fault with the occupation. I had a different viewpoint. I disliked the fakery practiced in my office, which, in addition to producing the *Pennsylvania News*, was expected to carry out public relations, publicity, and promotion.

One such deceptive practice concerned the arrival of celebrities on the Pennsylvania Railroad trains to Chicago. Now and then a prominent movie actress would somehow manage to avoid the press and arrive incognito. Distress then would be great in the office, and we would send a form, emblazoned with the railway's symbols, saying that so-and-so would be arriving on the Broadway Limited or whatever name train it was, when, and where. Then, with the help of the actress's press agent, we would drive her to Englewood Station about 45 minutes outside the Chicago Loop, put her on another incoming train in a compartment already packed with flowers, and the reporters, feature writers, and photographers would greet her as she stepped off the train at Union Station, apparently a bit weary after a transcontinental trip.

Also, I disliked the boredom of marking and listing all mentions of our trains in the Chicago and other papers sent to us for checking from on the line. These figures were totaled each week and reported to the New York offices of Ivy Ledbetter Lee, a pioneer and prominent public relations counsel often called the dean of the business. The Pennsylvania Railroad was one of his accounts.

Nor was that all: I was uncomfortable with the autocratic methods of our chief editor, Kenneth D. Pulcipher, who ran the Union Station office more like a military establishment than an editorial room. One of his favorite practices was to ask the staff to work Saturday afternoons although there was nothing important to be done.

To these experiences, guardedly related, I added those I learned from friends working on the house publications in other industries since I belonged to associations of such writers and editors. I answered the article, titling it, "House Organ Discords." But I was too craven to sign it with my own name. I chose Fred Welch, which contains my initials at least. After all, I was young, newly married, and could not afford to lose my job. It was 1930 and an economic depression was imminent. At least I was not paid by *The Quill.*

But that was not the end.

Not long after the July 31 issue (with my article) was received by subscribers, our editor could be heard expostulating over something in his roomy private office. Soon he called us all in. *All* included an assistant editor, a secretary/women's

editor, and my timid self, then titled editorial assistant.
Pulcipher railed against the article's author as he waved the
magazine at us, saying he wished he knew who the idiot was. I
remained silent but also amused, for the writer of the piece
stood right before him. My silence has been to my shame ever
since.

At some time or other, journalists and other writers have to
make such a choice: to be quiet and safe or to own up and take
the consequences. Fear of failure, I am afraid, was stronger
than conscience that day. It was a long time before I told my
wife of my cowardice.

She understood, as I knew she would. She naturally was
aware of our financial straits and my unwillingness to appeal to
my mother or stepfather for aid if I did get fired. It was
Bernice's salary that got us past many a tight spot.

She was Bernice Mather Browne, descended through her
mother from the New England Mathers (Richard and his two
sons, Increase and Cotton. Richard was a British clergyman; his
sons were American Puritan clergymen and writers). She never
boasted of the connection, however. I learned from her to be
more gentle, patient, and kindly with others. I also learned
much religious idealism from her that has guided my life ever
since and especially at times of stress before and after her death
in 1980.

Publicity and the church

My work in public relations, such as I did with the
Pennsylvania Railroad, soon extended to churches and religious
organizations.

The opportunity came about through my affiliation with
Ernest Tittle and the First Methodist Church. It was my offer of
stewardship, to volunteer my journalistic training and experience at its service. So in the early 1930s I was accepted to
guide the office staff in setting up a plan that would supply more
news releases to the surrounding media and make preparation of
the *First Church Review*, the eight-by-ten-inch, four-to-six-
page weekly, a bit more professional.

To be asked to do this planning may seem commonplace
today. Fifty years ago, however, individual churches rarely
organized their publicity and public relations activities system-
atically. They had no skilled persons to draw upon—or so they

thought. This hit home one day when I was talking to the pastor of a church of about 900 members in a city of about 200,000. We were discussing how congregations like his might call more public attention to their programs and activities.

"My trouble," he said, "is that I have not a single person in my church who could even serve on a publicity committee."

"Oh, but you have," I said. "You have Howard Palmer, the manager of the state press association and a former newspaperman. He would make a fine publicity committee member. He's been a faithful churchman all his life."

The pastor admitted that he did not know that.

"You also have a newspaper publisher." That, too, was news to him.

But nothing was done through the rest of that sleepy pastor's ministry in that city.

Admittedly, in those days publicity and public relations were not as prominent in the field of communications as they have become in the last quarter of this century. The church did its useful labors with little public recognition, often with misunderstanding, and certainly with far less outreach than it deserved.

The program at the Evanston church proved that church publicity planning can be contagious. The scheme I set up came to wider attention in the church press as well as locally.

What was done was simple enough. Each church organization was asked to appoint a publicity committee, even if only one person. The scrapbooks kept are evidence that the system worked. Most of the committee members were housewives, since they could organize their own time. In those years far fewer women worked outside their homes than do today.

These circle members were called together for a three-session workshop in news gathering and writing, with emphasis on writing. They caught on to news writing form and style quickly and were dependable, if a little unimaginative, about seeing a story. The classes were held in a church school classroom because I could put news story diagrams and other visual materials on blackboards. Such training periods were offered each fall thereafter for some years.[1]

1. The full text of the plan as well as a press chairman's manual developed to go with it, appears as appendix I in my book, *Interpreting the Church Through Press and Radio*, pp. 301-36.

Soon the church offices were flooded with copy. Enough was provided not only for the *Review* but also, since 10 to 15 copies of each release were provided, to supply the outside press and other media. Some required small textual adjustments. Stamped envelopes were prepared in advance. I had talked with editorial people ahead of time, telling them of the plan and what would be sent to them regularly.

Not that the system worked smoothly all the time. Now and then the joints creaked. Some chairmen became ill and turned in nothing; others simply lost interest or never understood the need for reliability. Others overlooked useful stories. But, in general, they turned in properly prepared copy and lots of it. The plan is usable to this day, with changes in specific publications to be reached and the addition of television offices.

This venture led to requests from the Vacation Church Schools, Bible Study groups, and other Evanston religious organizations for help on their publicity problems. Some years later, when I became a journalism teacher, I was invited to teach courses in church publicity at what is now Garrett-Evangelical Theological Seminary in Evanston. In time, similar courses were taught at Candler Seminary, Emory University, and Syracuse University.[2]

A return to Medill, teaching begins

As the depression years of the 1930s came closer, I realized that I would need more training in these and other phases of communications if I was to qualify for higher responsibilities. So I began to study for a master's degree in journalism at Medill.

Helping to pay the tuition was my first journalism teaching. I taught in two institutions in 1933-34: Englewood Evening High School's adult education program on Chicago's South Side, and Mundelein, a Catholic college for girls located just south of Evanston in Chicago. I was hired to teach newswriting and news editing at both. The high school stint meant a 70-mile round-trip by elevated trains; Mundelein I could reach by bus in 45 minutes, so it was less onerous. And the students were more responsive.

2. In contrast to those days in the 1930s is the encouraging sign of church progress today in the denominations, mainline or other, that have organized to tell their story to their various publics.

When I walked into the first meeting of my class at Mundelein I faced an unusual experience. I was not to realize what was happening to me until two semesters had passed. It was an occurrence not common in universities and colleges; at least it never was repeated in my own career, and I have not heard of it in others'. I was engaged as a lecturer for two semesters. I was the only man on the faculty: the other teachers were sisters of the order that operated the college, named for a distinguished cardinal.

About 20 young women enrolled in my news writing class that fall. Seated at the back of the room was a sister in full habit, serving as chaperone. That day and on all the succeeding days she wrote a great deal, no doubt letters to fill this boring time for her. The same guardian of my students' morals sat through the second semester course on news editing.

My contract was not renewed for the next year. Since I was expecting to get a full-time newspaper job I was not concerned. But I was interested to see, when the new Mundelein catalog was issued, if my courses had been dropped. On the contrary. Both were being offered. And there was the new teacher—the gentle and kindly chaperone. She had been taking notes of my lectures and keeping examples of the lab exercises I used.

We have since corresponded; she now teaches elsewhere. Only a few years ago we met once more and laughed over the incident, which I still consider somewhat cunning. But there was a gain, after all. One of my first books, *The Copyreader's Workshop*, written with H. F. Harrington, was published the next year. It was based largely on a tryout of my materials in the Mundelein editing course. So this stint at the college gave me both teaching experience and material for a book.

From city editor to faculty member

My master's degree completed, with a double major in journalism and political science, I was ready to return to active journalism. The opportunity came when Curtis D. MacDougall became editor of the Evanston *Daily News-Index*, an old daily. MacDougall, now retired from Northwestern's faculty, was to become one of the most noted teachers in U.S. journalism education. His text on news reporting and writing has led the field for half a century. I was hired as a reporter, became a copy editor, and then city editor.

The call to become a full-time journalism teacher came after I had taught a Medill summer session course on newspaper feature writing in 1937. Three years at the *Daily News-Index* (at times its detractors called it the *Daily New Insect*) were enough for me by then and the taste of part-time teaching at the university level was pleasing. Full time, I thought, could be still more so. And it was.

Teachers and showmen

Teachers often are frustrated actors, and I suppose I was like all the rest, but I did not become a showman teacher.

Perhaps this was unfortunate because the entertainers draw the largest class attendance and therefore the larger salaries and quicker promotions. One example of this breed of educators, William Montgomery McGovern, was an expert on the politics of Southeast Asia. He had saved his salmon-colored robes from one of his trips and appeared in classes in them now and then. He also liked wearing them at faculty social functions. The only show business academic who outdid Dr. McGovern was at another university where I was to each later. This professor used to dress in sequined motorcycling garb and chug and snort her way into the classroom on her cycle. The nearest I came to

While I was city editor of the Daily News-Index *(green eyeshades were in vogue then), we were visited occasionally by school children on field trips.*

being a performer was to stage a laboratory exercise involving shrunken heads of the Ecuadorean Jivaro tribe. These I had been given by a former student returning from South America.

After the usual apprenticeship of teaching newswriting and editing, I became an assistant professor, specializing in feature writing and magazine article writing courses. Finally I graduated into advanced writing, journalism history, magazine journalism and publishing, and critical writing for the press. I also became more and more interested in the contribution journalism could make to religion. Several times I proposed a program or sequence in religion journalism for the clergy and people with the ambition to be religion journalists. But there was no interest in the idea. It was not to die, however.

The art of teaching writing

The advanced writing course permitted me to do a little pioneering with teaching techniques and exposing the students earlier than perhaps any others at the time to some developments in simplified writing styles. I learned that students were grateful for line-by-line criticism of their writing, and thus I asked them to type line numbers into their copy; I issued a set of symbols that I wrote beside a line to save myself the trouble of writing the same correction or advice over and over. For example, *CQ* next to a line or segment questions its accuracy; that symbol is used by news services to their bureaus. I did not go so far, however, as a colleague in the English department who later achieved radio fame, Bergan Evans. He had a score of rubber stamps made that carried his concise remarks, and merely stamped them into place where suitable, usually in the margins.

All this fuss was necessary because even as far back as the 1930s, high school and college students had a sickness from which they still suffer today. It is a disease that the youth of the 1980s also have contracted. They did not know how to spell correctly, their writing was obscure and involved, and they liked overlong words and sentences. To find that their own students were ill in this manner was especially frustrating to journalism teachers since their pupils were expected to be impeccable in such matters. Various degrees of illiteracy were not so important for engineers, mathematicians, or scientists, but for neophyte writers to be incapable of writing a clear sentence was disgraceful.

Along came a teacher, however, who did something about the problem. He was Rudolf Flesch of the Columbia University faculty. He published *The Art of Plain Talk* in 1946 during my last full year of teaching at Medill. That book tackled the problem of cloudy, imprecise writing with a simple formula based on the study and treatment of sentences. Flesch built on the work of scholars before him. The difference was that they worked in obscurity while his book went into the best-seller status almost at once. Those who have followed Flesch, building on his work, have also become popular.

I was using another textbook in my Advanced Writing Practice class but abandoned it in midsemester to adopt Flesch's, to the benefit of students who applied his formula. His advice was taken seriously by major newspapers and the news agencies. Some professionals pooh-poohed his counsel largely because they misunderstood it. He was accused of making all sentences the same length and of reducing everyone's vocabulary to a short list of words, neither of which was true. He and later scholars were good medicine for the media's language ills.

Certainly my students benefited. My pride in them has been great, and I have derived great satisfaction from their accomplishments. Some are far more talented than I and have accomplished vastly more. One is Clifford B. Hicks, who has been editor in chief of *Popular Mechanics* and is now one of its chief book editors. Another is James W. Carty, Jr., one of the earliest persons in the USA to be ordained to the Christian ministry as a religion journalist. For many years he has been chairman or professor in the journalism department of Bethany College, Bethany, West Virginia, and also is an author and a linguist who has worked in foreign countries under religion or secular educational sponsorship.

Kuldip Nayer of India, another student, was editor of several of his country's leading English-language dailies, active in national politics, and is an author of books on public affairs. Roberta Applegate, after some years in secular journalism that included staff positions on the *Miami Herald*, joined the Kansas State University faculty and rose to a professorship in the school of journalism. Robert H. Estabrook, now editor and publisher of the *Lakeville Journal* in Connecticut, before that was United

The class in news reporting and writing at Northwestern had an elaborate fieldwork program in which students covered stories and turned them in to me as, in effect, city editor.

Nations correspondent for the *Washington Post*; he also was that paper's chief editorial writer.

Others of my students have become newspaper executives, magazine editors, writers for or staff members of scores of publications, correspondents, free-lancers, columnists, and successful in a number of media where I did no teaching, such as advertising, photography, and the graphic arts; still others are in journalism teaching.

End of the line at Northwestern

I remained at Northwestern until 1946. Then my teaching there ended under unhappy circumstances. The early 1940s when the U.S. was in World War II was not the best time to take the pacifist position. But as I have already stated, my convictions were rooted in my religious beliefs. These I had held two decades before the war as a member of the Fellowship of Reconciliation, the War Resister's League, and other organizations committed to nonviolent solutions of international and other conflicts.

Besides my problematical status as a conscientious objector, promotion and accompanying salary increases were being denied me because I lacked the Ph.D. degree. By then, though, I had published, alone or as coauthor, five books, all in the communications field, as well as several hundred articles and reviews in professional journals, the press of religion, and other special subjects. This publishing, it seemed to me, should balance my lack of a terminal degree, as the doctorate is called in academia, as if to say without a terminal degree you may be terminated.[3]

At any rate, for whatever reasons, the Northwestern administration pressured me to resign and my contract was terminated after the spring semester of 1946. In 1951, after I had been at Syracuse for five years, Northwestern offered me the increase in rank and salary denied earlier. But Syracuse had done too much for me by then to leave it for this offer.

3. Perhaps the fact that Albright College in Reading, Pennsylvania, conferred an honorary Litt.D. degree upon me in 1955, for my services to journalism and to religion journalism in particular, acted as a buffer in my later career.

6   Working Writer

On reviewing books. Motives of a religious writer. Working habits. How the writer's task was accomplished.

My own writing did not stop when I moved with my boxes of books that crowded fall day in 1951 from Northwestern to work in the magazine department at Syracuse. As early as 1933, I had been writing more than 50 book reviews a year. Most were for *Quill and Scroll* magazine, the national quarterly of the Quill and Scroll Society, an honorary organization of high school journalists in the USA with headquarters first at Northwestern and later at the University of Iowa. I was added to the staff during the Northwestern connection and have been on its masthead ever since.

Editors responsible for book review pages and sections have to choose between two options about how they will run such portions of the newspaper or magazine. Should they do all the reviewing themselves or parcel out the books to experts? If they review everything themselves they run the risk of posing as experts on all topics and forms. But to do that is much less work than is the other method. If they depend upon experts they must assemble a list of reviewers to whom they can turn dependably. Then they must wrap and mail the books to them and wait for the reviews to come back, which may or may not always be on time. The quality of the criticism probably will be higher, however, since the guest reviewers are more likely to know what they are writing about.

I chose a combination plan. Those books in areas where I think I am sufficiently competent, I handle myself; others, I send to a staff reviewer depending upon the topic. These are mainly high school, college, or university teachers or people in the field doing the work described by the book, for example.

During my half century of reviewing so far I have been outspoken, as have most of my guest reviewers. I do not tell these outside reviewers what to say or think about the books they have agreed to criticize, nor do I edit their copy beyond correcting technical or factual errors. My own reviews sometimes are complimentary of a book, sometimes denunciatory, but usually balanced, pointing out strong and weak points alike. Perhaps that is why, after so many years, few complaints have reached me. Either that, or the editors have not told me of the complaints. Since they continue to keep me on the staff, however, the assumption is that the complaints have not been overwhelming.

I do recall one that came from a parochial schoolteacher who scolded me because she thought the language in a certain book was in bad taste and thus the book should not have been reviewed. That brought up the matter of whether only "good" books should be reviewed. I do not agree; readers, should be warned against books that are not "good." But by "good" I mean not merely a matter of taste but whether the book is false in its premises or faulty in its statements of fact, guilty of gross errors or of extremely bad writing.

One author complained mildly at my suggestions for strengthening the textbook he had written. But when he brought out a new edition several years later, I compared the two versions when reviewing the new one and noticed that he had accepted some of the criticisms. The only time I came close to being in possibly serious trouble was when I reviewed a book whose treatment of its subject was so inflammatory I insinuated that the writing seemed that of a crazed person. That brought a letter from a lawyer threatening a libel suit if there was not an apology. I agreed that it was the writing I should have reflected upon, and not its author, and published a retraction.

Perhaps my reviews and those of my guest writers are less penetrating than I think they are. More likely, however, is the tone of the reviews—while candid, the adverse criticisms are not expressed sarcastically or caustically. Possibly this is because I have written books myself and know all the work involved in producing them. I am a believer in the book as an important communications and educational tool.

In a day when electronic communications dominate, I continue to fight for the salvation of the book as a medium. Reviewing books and giving them a place of importance is an effort in that direction. This loyalty to books, however, does not mean that reading just any book is worth doing. Too many popular books set up false standards—the sentimental novels that lead the list of what women, in Western nations at least, wish to read, for example. The innumerable how-to books—health, marriage, moneymaking, sex, and popular psychology—often do more harm than not reading a book at all.

Journalism and the religion writer

During the first five years at Syracuse, my own book writing accelerated. Laurence Campbell and I had collaborated while I was at Northwestern (he was teaching elsewhere) on a basic introductory text called *Exploring Journalism* (New York: Prentice-Hall, 1943). It was a successful general text. Living near each other in Syracuse for a year while we both were on the university faculty gave us an opportunity to plan a second edition, which appeared in 1949. *Newsmen at Work* (Boston: Houghton Mifflin) appeared the same year. Two years later I published my first book on the magazine field (*The Magazine World*, New York: Prentice-Hall). If this number of books seems like extraordinary productivity it must be remembered that I was teaching courses in each area and was able to try out my chapters in the classrooms and laboratories.

In 1951 I published my first book relating to religion and communications, *Interpreting the Church Through Press and Radio*. This book reflected my continuing interest in religion writing—not only in producing books, but also in preparing courses at the university and training programs for religion journalists.

The fact is, however, that though I am a religious writer, I actually do not write much about religion. That is, I am a religious person but do not write about theology, denominationalism, church history, evangelism, or any other aspect of religion except its use of the media of mass communication.

This distinction gradually is becoming more widely recognized, not of course about me but about certain other persons who write about religion and church, especially journalists. The Religion Newswriters Association for most of its years has been known as the Religious Newswriters Association. Yet some members of the group of reporters make no pretense of being religious, that is, of practicing any particular religion. Some have little interest in the subject and may even be atheists or agnostics.

Police reporters, for example, at times are shifted to the religion beat as a sort of punishment for inefficiency, a practice more typical of the past than the present. But when reporters are shifted from police, county, or other beats that are considered respected news centers, they tend to be resentful. That does not make for fair coverage of religion or the churches. City or metropolitan editors never would think of putting an enemy of the sciences on the science beat or a hater of the law system on the courthouse run.

During my school days in Reading, Pennsylvania, reporters like myself were made responsible for the church news. This again showed little understanding on the part of the editors that such specialized news needs, not beginners to cover it, but experienced news gatherers. It also revealed lack of interest in and respect for such news.

Such assignments are similar to the still common practice of filling key editorial positions on denominational publications with pastors or other church-connected persons who have not the slightest knowledge of communications, journalism, or publishing. Both nonreligious, unreligious, and religiously uneducated religion reporters and religious folk devoid of knowledge of and interest in communications are misfits. Sometimes the religion writers become sincerely religious after contact with the church world and other times they resign in disgust at what they see occurring in that world. Similarly, the church publication editors learn their new profession in time and do well at it or drop out after making many mistakes at the expense of staff and readers.

So readers of this book should understand the nature of my religious professions. I have been a churchman for many years, have tried to serve my beliefs and my denomination in many ways, and to serve other religious groups through my abilities, such as they are, as journalist, author, and teacher. I have interests and beliefs which in general coincide with those of my denomination. If I did not I could not labor so long and willingly in the realm of religion, for it would bore me.

But I do not pretend to be capable of writing about theology, apologetics, doctrine, or other such basic topics. My obligation is to help religious persons to learn more about the world of religion, to distinguish one faith from another, to be more tolerant of those faiths but not to be blind to their faults. My obligation is also to help these persons equip themselves to write about religion so that whatever they say is said clearly and fairly, without regard to creed.

Book writing—hard labor in print

A leave of absence to teach in India (see next chapter) did not interrupt my book writing. In fact, it accelerated it, for I had new subjects. And thus it has gone through my writing career: new activities and interests lead to new subjects for books.

Those books and the more than a dozen that have followed since have often led fellow teachers and aspiring authors to ask if I hired researchers to assist me. Or if I have some secret for effortless book writing.

I have had no help and no benefit of secret methods. Until recently I always have done all the work on the books I have written alone. I myself type all drafts of a manuscript or whatever I am responsible for in a collaboration. Although Bernice was willing to help and was expert at the typewriter, I could not accept her aid. For I change the writing down to the last minute and insert new ideas and ways of saying what I want to say up to the day the script is sent to the publisher. One must stop work on any piece of writing sometime, but even after an article or a book is published I can find new ways to improve it.

This constant revision of my work used to trouble me. Then Fred Demarest, head of the Newhouse photography department, pointed out that just as I do not hesitate to discard inferior photo negatives or prints or slides so I should be just as willing to throw out words and sentences.

While producing the books, I also was writing and publishing hundreds of free-lance articles and an occasional short story in the secular as well as religion press in the USA, India,

Sweden, and other countries. Several of the books were translated into Hindi or Spanish.

The reasons for my apparent productivity are simple. My home life was plain: no children or other relatives were about. We did not play bridge or spend much time at movie houses or watching television. We did not ignore the electronic media but neither were we addicts. I seem to need less sleep than some other persons, often making do with five or six hours. While I was teaching I organized my time to have some free every day for my professional writing, doubling up the next day if I missed any part of the quota. I have an extensive library, most of it on my special subjects; it includes 12 two-, three-, or four-tier file cabinets, most of them with four drawers. These contain photographs, negatives, various types of documents, clippings, letters, and other materials, all in labeled folders.

Space is a major factor. My study has never been large

The floor-to-ceiling library at home contains more than 1,000 books, but I must constantly weed that garden of words to make room for new publications.

enough. The floor-to-ceiling book shelving around three sides of the library contains more than 1,000 books, but I must constantly weed that garden of words to make room for new publications. I usurp other rooms: the dining room table should display my Norwegian and Swedish crystal; instead it is covered with unanswered letters and manuscripts in progress. The small fruit room in the basement does not contain fruit, but piles of runs of magazines that I cannot find at libraries. Others of that kind are in the garage cupboards. Nor is that all. In the office I use at the university is another file case of source materials and beside it more books.

Orderliness, which I do not assert I have in my working methods, is an important element also. I would do more and better work if I could keep up with my filing system. A writer must choose between keeping his materials in order and doing the necessary stints at the word processor, typewriter, or the writing pad. For my type of work—all nonfiction, factual material—operating a thorough filing system that involves photographs, clippings, letters, formal documents, and reports is too time-consuming if done methodically. The only other way to handle such a glut of collectibles is to hire an assistant or to turn to computer storage, neither of which is practical for college professors and run-of-the-mill writers and probably suitable only for authors of international best sellers.

Because I have written so much in the midst of piles of unfiled paper and film, some of my friends think writing comes easily for me. As my various editors at publishing houses know, including the publishers of this book, this idea is untrue. I still need to revise and rewrite as much as any neophyte. Each book or article is a challenge. The writing itself is hard work enough. Digging out facts is taxing labor, physically tiring and often boring, but necessary. Some authors compare writing to detective work. But I never have wanted to be a detective.

Then why was all this work done? Why, deep in my retirement years, do I continue?

Because I believe I have something to say. And the only way I can express it is through writing, having no talent as musician, sculptor, painter, or any other kind of creative artist. That is my motive. I find that the work is just as hard as with any other motive, such as making money or inflating the ego.

7   Teaching and Writing in the New India

An experiment in cross-cultural journalism education, writing, and publishing.

In 1951, when the magazine department at Syracuse was firmly established, I was asked if I would be willing to go to India to help launch a department of journalism in one of the constituent Christian colleges of Nagpur University. With my long interest in Mohandas Gandhi and the history of India, I accepted. By the time my passage to India actually began in early 1952, three additional professional reasons for going had been added.

One was to encourage more persons to prepare reading materials useful in Frank Laubach's "Each One Teach One" literacy campaign. Another was to produce books and articles that might develop from my stay in that country. A third and less important reason was related to authorship and journalism: to give Indian writers an opportunity to contribute to a leading American magazine, *Reader's Digest*.

The major goals were accomplished with one degree or other of success. But the minor aim was a failure. The experience gives some insight into the status of journalists of India then and now.

Realizing that I would need to know far more than I did about India and its communications systems in particular, I asked the State Department for early departure from the USA.

That way I could travel throughout the subcontinent to visit editors, publications offices, and printing plants of both newspapers and magazines. To prepare for the books and articles that I would write, I signed certain writing contracts before departure. One was a book for Friendship Press in New York on India's social problems. My *Face to Face with India* was one of a series of study books to be out in 1954. I also had arranged to write a series on our journey and life in India for the *Syracuse Post-Standard*, the large morning daily.

Two days before sailing from New York in February 1952, I stopped at Pleasantville, New York, for a conference with five editorial members of *Reader's Digest*.[1] They were interested in learning about writers from India who could provide articles about that country, either for the major U.S. edition or the India edition.

When I came to know possible contributors to the magazine several months later in India, I explained the opportunity, noting that payment for one article would be as much as Rs. 5,000 (about U.S. $1,000 in those days, equivalent to the annual salary of some Indian journalists then). I suggested topics, noted the writers' names and dossiers, and asked them to clear with me first at Hislop College in Nagpur.

The venture failed, I feel, not because I did not try, but because the journalists I encountered lacked time, drive, or competence to take advantage of what was a remarkable opportunity. And I met many, on publications of all sizes and types. Not even the huge fees for which the *Digest* is so noted moved them to their writing pads, even to querying.

In the 14 months I was in India, only two writers responded. Both suggested off-the-top-of-the-head ideas showing no in-depth thinking or investigation and little familiarity with the magazine, much less with the editor of their own country's edition. What this experience taught me was that the lack of initiative or ability was typical of much of the quality of India's journalists of the early 1950s, with the exception of a few outstanding writers.

The evidence was compelling. Later, I put some of it into articles in Indian publications, bringing upon myself a repri-

1. These were Ralph Henderson, managing editor, who was the first staff member hired by DeWitt Wallace, founder of the magazine in 1925; Charles Ferguson, William Hard, Jr., Harry Harper, and Ralph O'Keefe

mand from Chester Bowles, then U.S. ambassador to India. He naturally did not want someone getting State Department grants to be candid about certain conditions in the Indian press, no matter how tactfully put. But some editors told me that such criticism was in order.

Bound for India

When my wife, Bernice, and I boarded ship at the Holland America Line's docks, on February 6 in Hoboken, New Jersey, this search for writers, the visiting of publications offices, tourism, and opportunities for service were still ahead of us. I had been looking forward eagerly to the journey. It meant more sea life, for we were sure to travel in four different passenger liners on the round-trip. Our first was the *Ryndam*, bound for London. After two weeks in the United Kingdom and France, we sailed by another vessel, the *Strathnaver*, to India, through the Suez Canal.

On board we came to know people of India, including two young men from Calcutta, Kanai Chandra Paul and Monotosh Mookerjee, whom we later visited in their city; Kanai still writes. They reminded us of the comic strip pair, Mutt and Jeff, one tall and gawky, the other short and dumpy. Eager to talk about India and America, they discussed Mohandas Gandhi often. (I had read Gandhi's *An Autobiography* and Louis Fischer's life of him.) Through Kanai and Monotosh we were introduced to books by one of India's most important writers, Nirad C. Chaudhuri. His new book then, *The Autobiography of an Unknown Indian*, was being discussed widely in India, as we learned on our tour of the country. It had been published only a few months before.

Other shipboard reading on the voyage included James Bryce's *India on the Threshold* and the one important historical work, Margarita Barns's *The Indian Press*, published in England. For relaxation, I read Anthony Trollope's *Barchester Towers*.

Bombay and Indian journalists

India came in sight on March 15. As the *Strath* hove broadside to the pier, we spotted Vimala Rajamanikam (now Mrs. Christy Arangaden) standing amidst the piles of crates, rows of cranes, and thick coiled ropes. Vimala had earned her master's in journalism the year before and now was editing a Christian magazine for children. With her were four others—two representatives of the Intermission offices there; Ruth Ure, an American missionary on the National Christian Council staff at Nagpur; and a Miss Saur of the United States Information Services (USIS) in Bombay.

We were driven through jammed streets in a USIS car piled high with our luggage, and were left at a Methodist missionary hostel at 22 Clubback Road. In a few days we gained an overall picture of Bombay: streets crowded night and day, new tall buildings going up next to ramshackle ones, many people looking poor and miserable. Cows had the right-of-way, and crows and vultures roosted in the trees or on buildings.

I met my first professional Indian journalist on his own ground thanks to two medical doctor friends, Eddie and Piloo Bharucha, whom we had met on the trip over. He was S. Natarajan, as he signed everything, editor of the *Bombay Chronicle*, then a leading English language daily (now defunct). Natarajan was equally widely known for his editorship of the *Indian Social Reformer*. "Nat," as friends called him, subsequently wrote the chapter on editorial writing for the book I later edited on journalism in India.

My tour of India's publishing enterprises ranged from New Delhi in the North and Calcutta in the East to Madras in the South, Bombay in the West, and smaller cities in between. One of the most able of the editors I came to know during this tour was Frank Moraes, chief of the leading Indian daily, the *Times of India*. An Anglo-Indian, he was heavyset and coldly self-confident. But like all his peers, with a few exceptions, he had not the slightest knowledge of what a journalism department's function is within a university.

As the degree of ignorance of this matter was revealed from city to city, my own temperature rose with that of the country, which was swinging between 90 and 105 degrees Fahrenheit every day. The disdain of the professionals reminded me of the old days of journalism teaching in the U.S., when editors generally ridiculed the new subject.

I was moved by the similar Indian reaction to write articles on what journalism education is and what was being planned for Hislop. I appealed to the editors' national pride, sense of fairness, and aroused their interest by sharing my plans with them. Articles about these plans appeared widely in the Indian press during the following months. Among the publications using them was the leading periodical, the *Illustrated Weekly of India*. They were also picked up by the *Hindustan Times* of New Delhi, *Nagpur Times*, *Careers Today*, the *Statesman*, Delhi, and numerous others, some of them translated for vernacular publications.

The tour equipped me better to help my students understand the extent and nature of India's press. India's journalism education at that time was limited to a few private schools in the big cities. It was restricted to technical training of questionable quality and to three university programs that offered little journalism and a great deal of history, economics, and political science.

Nagpur, City of Snakes

We arrived in Nagpur, at the center of India, after one of the most comfortable train journeys of the many we were to make. It was so, despite the dust coming through the frames of the rattling windows, because we had wide berths, new bedrolls, two overhead fans that revolved slowly, and our own toilet facilities.

As our train steamed into the station at Nagpur (meaning City of Snakes), we were met by Dr. David Moses, principal of Hislop Christian College, which was sponsoring the first journalism department in independent India. Dr. Moses was a leader in the Christian movement in his country and later to come to worldwide recognition as one of the presidents of the World Council of Churches. In the mid-1950s, he was invited to be the Henry R. Luce visiting professor of theology at Union Theological Seminary in New York.[2] He was knowledgeable about the religions of India and an author of books about religion, but he did not let himself speak disparagingly of the Hindus, Moslems, nor the followers of the many other faiths to be found in his country.

From faculty colleagues I learned that one morning, a few weeks before we arrived in Nagpur, Dr. Moses came to the college to be greeted by panicked students shouting that there

2. Luce was the founder of Time, Inc., a major American magazine and book publisher.

was a cobra in the compound. He marched to his office, took a rifle from its wall rack, walked to the area where the students were assembled in awe, and with one shot blew off the snake's waving head. This was no legend.

Others who came to greet us were several Nagpur University and other college officers, including Ruth Ure, the American missionary we had met in Bombay. As an official of the National Christian Council, she had worked diligently to bring about the Hislop College journalism department. She had also done much to make my invitation to teach in India possible.

We were duly garlanded with flowers and driven to the National Christian Council lodge within the Civil Lines, that is, the area of the city where, under British rule, public officials generally resided. There we were given large quarters, a bearer (butler is the closest translation but otherwise there is little resemblance) named Makhu, and a *chowkidar*, or night watchman, who coughed lightly if we came home after dark so we'd know he was on duty.

Although it had 440,000 inhabitants, Nagpur was more like a giant village than a metropolis. Buildings were mainly one story high, mostly jerry-built. Streets were unpaved in most areas, and, of course, choked with people, skinny dogs, chawing goats, scrawny cows, lumbering water buffalo, a few cars, innumerable bicycles, wood carts drawn by man or animal, rickshaws, and vendors' stalls at street sides.

Commodities were hard to find, at least for Americans used to package goods, fresh or frozen vegetables, frozen meats, and dainty bakery items. Later we found groups of stalls in other areas of the city, in principle like the malls of Western cities. We finally did most of our shopping and marketing in a nearby emporium owned by Muslims that specialized in the needs of Westerners or the better-heeled Indians.

The housing problems we faced when we first went to Syracuse were in a way repeated in Nagpur. The "blocks," as our new home setting was called, were not yet ready on our arrival. These can be likened to an American motel: buildings one story high, with common side walls, stretching for two city blocks. While we waited for ours, we stayed at the National Christian Council headquarters all summer because the Roland Scotts were in the hill country to escape Nagpur's ghastly heat. We, too, would escape it by and by, when the temperatures

reached 120 degrees Fahrenheit, and flee to the town of
Kodaikanal, in the Kodai Hills of South India.

A new program at Hislop

Dr. Moses briefed me on the Hislop educational programs
and sought my plans for forming the new department. In India
under Britain, before the formation of Pakistan, there had been
one department of journalism in Lahore. But I did not follow its
model, for it was characterized by all the traditional practices.[3]
Great emphasis on memorization and long but infrequent ex-
aminations on which the final mark depend are two examples.

To avoid this approach, the principal of Hislop and I agreed
on following a partly American pattern. I wished for some
innovations, such as laboratory sessions (sans typewriters, however, for there was no money for them), frequent short tests,
fieldwork, internships, compulsory class attendance, individual
student counseling, and class discussion periods. All this he

*Seventy-five percent of my students at Hislop College were
men. The women members needed more direction, usually because few had had the same practical experience.*

3. The Lahore journalism department, as a matter of fact, was revived in India to
become the Department of Journalism at Panjab University in New Delhi. In July 1962
it was shifted to Chandigarh where it still operates as Department of Communication,
Panjab University, Chandigarh.

liked, having visited U.S. colleges. But it required approval by the Nagpur University administration, of which Hislop was only one of almost 50 units. I had to appear before the governing body and plead my case. Eventually, it all was approved.

Before leaving the USA, I had searched for possible textbooks to use in my Hislop courses. I wanted textbooks by writers from India, but found not one in any of their languages. Biographies, critical studies, memoirs, histories, law studies, vocational advice, government annual reports on the press, and yearbooks there were. But not books giving thorough instruction on newswriting, reporting, editing, magazine article writing, graphic arts, editorial writing, or the many other facets of journalism.

I shipped more than 100 of the books from my personal library, including about 10 British texts, although the U.K., with only one journalism school at the time, had produced only a modest practical literature on the subject. But I thought these 10 useful since the Indian press, especially the dominant English language publications, for years have been strongly influenced by British writing style, makeup, and typography.

The Hislop library had one book on journalism in India, a volume of reminiscences by an obscure newsman. I rushed off orders to U.S. publishers, meantime putting my own copies on reserve with misgivings about their survival. But I need not have worried. Many I left for the library.

This absence of indigenous texts moved me to do something about filling the gap. My tour of India also having verified the lack of such texts, I proposed to a large Bombay firm the possibility of issuing a general book to be edited and partly written by me but mostly by experts in the Indian press scene in 1952. P. D. Tandon of Allahabad or P.D.T., as he was always addressed by me and others who knew him, was one of the 12 contributors.[4]

Author or editor of some two dozen books, Tandon was for many years correspondent in Allahabad for the *National Herald*

---

4. See Roland E. Wolseley, editor and coauthor, *Journalism in Modern India* (Bombay: Asia Publishing House, 1953). The second revised edition (Bombay and New York, 1964) was distributed in the USA by Taplinger. Contributors included an editor of one of the largest English dailies; the superintendent of the Baptist Mission Press; S. (for Swaminath) Natarajan, a writer for U.S. and U.K. dailies and author of books on America and India; and the editor of a vernacular daily. The introduction was by the president of the All-India Newspaper Editors Conference.

of Lucknow, then a leading English language daily founded by Jawaharlal Nehru, the first and famed prime minister of India. Though I was never able to actually meet him, I had thought of Tandon as a possible contributor to *Reader's Digest*. He was involved in so many other projects, however, that he was not interested nor did he need the financial incentive. Later, after I returned to Syracuse, we collaborated on a biography of Mohandas Gandhi[5] and a book on three emminent women of India including Kasturbai Gandhi.[6]

David Moses stood firmly behind my aims for the department at Hislop. He agreed to assign local journalists with adequate experience to handle highly specialized courses, such as law of the Indian press and graphic arts. In the latter the provincial government printing plant was used as a laboratory. The seven Nagpur daily newspapers, two of which were in English, took on a few interns and also arranged for student field trips to their plants. We also had their cooperation, as we did from several large national magazines, in sending visiting speakers. A number of these periodicals published articles I wrote about our pioneering program.

Dr. Moses also provided me with what I never had had at an American university, a private secretary. He was Varkey Cherian, a Christian Indian, a good student and an efficient secretary within the limits of the space and equipment available to him.

The college staff included my only full-time colleague at Hislop, Professor Harold A. Ehrensperger, an American journalist, teacher, and Methodist missionary. He had been the founding editor of *Motive*, an influential Methodist magazine for college age youth. His assignment with me was to provide the literacy portion of our curriculum. He had been engaged in such work north of Nagpur at Jabalpur, so it was not much of a shift for him. He was a long admirer and friend of the Laubach

5. P. D. Tandon and Roland E. Wolseley, *Gandhi: Warrior of Non-Violence* (New Delhi: National Book Trust, 1969). See also Tandon's *Flames from the Ashes: Memoirs of a Lone Traveller* (Allahabad, India: St. Paul's Press, 1981). We wanted Tandon's name first since he is an Indian and the book was to be marketed chiefly in India. He had known all of the protagonists, including Gandhi himself. He also is widely acquainted with the present Gandhi family (not related to the Mahatma), which included the late Indira Gandhi.
6. P. D. Tandon and Roland E. Wolseley, *Three Women to Remember* (Allahabad, India: St. Paul's Press, 1975). Covered in this edition are also Indira Gandhi and Sarojini Naidu. The 1982 Hindi edition, titled *Four Flames of Lamps*, included Machadevi Verma, the poet.

family and thoroughly familiar with the Laubach literacy methods and especially of the need for literature for new readers. We called his courses ones in ''social education,'' a euphemism for correction of illiteracy. That included study of and preparation of written and printed materials for use by villagers. Students applied the journalistic principles of the rest of the program where suitable.

Our program did not at first lead to a degree; it did eventually. But for the time being we decided to issue only a diploma and a certificate, the difference being in the amount and quality of work undertaken. Almost all students went for the diploma but not all were granted it.

The Hislop department in a few years inspired others to establish programs at a similar level in a few other universities. In the 30 years since Hislop's pioneering department was

Varkey Cherian (right) with Mrs. Cherian and their two sons. He was a good student as well as my secretary when I headed the new journalism program at Hislop College.

founded, 29 university-level journalism programs have been set up. Almost all continue to exist today. Several offer the bachelor's degree, a few the master's, and one the doctorate in communications or journalism.

A leading adviser of such departments was Dr. K. E. Eapen, a South Indian, who has a master's degree in journalism from Syracuse and a doctorate in communications from the University of Wisconsin. He was department head at Hislop and later at Bangalore and Kerala universities. Now retired, he is widely known for his research work in communications.

A smooth year—sort of

The academic year at Hislop went smoothly for an institution of its kind in India. No student strikes occurred. For me, there were diversions and new experiences as a teacher. I could not become accustomed to seeing students rise when I entered the classroom—with one student behind me who had come to my office early so he could carry my books and other materials. And they remained standing until I signaled them to be seated. Such respect for a professor was in sharp contrast to the casual classroom conduct in the USA.

Neither did I like the practice of women students' being segregated in a *zenana* section at the back of the room. So I alphabetized the seating of students, thus expediting taking roll and delighting all the students, especially the boys.

We had 42 students, from 15 different geographical areas of India. They spoke that many languages and dialects between them, and their only common tongue was English. Not all were as proficient in it as they should have been.

One of the least proficient gave me a major headache. He was N. O. George, who came to see me one June morning. He was quiet, mild-looking, a bit swarthy as South Indians often are. He dressed like all the other men students—wrinkled trousers and an open-collar shirt.

"I want to join the journalism course," he announced.

"Why do you want to do so?"

He ignored the question and insisted he would qualify.

I gave him a test assignment, to be turned in two days later. He was to write a 1,000-word descriptive feature on Nagpur as a city.

He turned his copy in on time, the three-page piece was

well typed, and it was smoothly written. On the strength of that, his experience, and his determination, we told him he could study for a certificate but not a diploma.

George's first laboratory test papers revealed that his English was at the level of a four-year-old in the USA. We questioned his well-phrased trial feature and learned that his brother, also at Hislop (this was the first news we had of him), and certain friends had helped George write it.

When we confronted him with these facts, he admitted that he had had help. We dropped the matter partly because he was better than many others in being prompt with his work, and he attended his classes faithfully. (This is an accomplishment in a country where class cutting is notorious since class lectures can be bought at the college bookstore.) Also, he pleaded sincerely for another chance.

One day a few months later, I was skimming a new Bombay publication, *Public Opinion*, issued by the publishers of a sensational pro-Communist and anti-American weekly, *Blitz*. To my astonishment, on an inside page appeared a one-column article saying that American teachers at Nagpur were an American fifth column, were attacking the USSR, and singing the praises of the ''American imperialists.'' It went on with few facts but much anti-American propaganda. Of their own accord, when this diatribe was read in classes, our students signed a reply, denying the charges. The denial was printed, unchanged.

Later we learned that George was a pawn for the Communist party in Nagpur (at that time the only one; now there are several such parties with differing ideologies). He was being visited by men at his hostel, and it was he who had fed *Public Opinion* all the garbled information about Hislop.

I talked with a USIS officer, who confirmed that one of the Communist party practices in India then was to urge young people to enroll in a college or university and deliberately do badly in their work so that they could stay on longer, making up deficiencies. In this way, they would have time to indoctrinate their peers.

As it turned out, George had plenty of time. Failing all his first term work, he was expelled. But a few days later we were notified by a Nagpur attorney that he was filing suit against Hislop College and me complaining of discrimination against his Communist views. The administration reluctantly reinstated

him under a special arrangement. At the end of the second term
N. O. George again was among the flunkers. I never learned
what became of him because my Fulbright term ended a few
months later.

Sunstroke, Srinagar, and Syracuse

Toward the end of that second and final term, the expected
monsoon rains did not come. Our water line—a single pipe
running along the rear of the houses, suspended from the
walls—allowed us to tap less and less water daily. The supply
was shut off by the municipality for a half day, then for ten
hours, finally there was only one half-hour flow a day.

One morning in early March 1953, it was so blisteringly
hot that I wore just sandals and shorts. "Only mad dogs and
Englishmen go out in the midday sun," Noel Coward said in
one of his songs, but so do some mad Americans. I stood there a
half hour in a line with my back to the sun and nothing on my
head. The water finally began to trickle, and I filled my
containers and carried them into the house in several trips. But
by evening I could not have lifted a thimbleful of water. I was
delirious. We called Dr. Peggy Martin, a missionary physician
at Muir Hospital in Nagpur. "Sunstroke," she said.

The attack couldn't have come at a worse time. It was
necessary to wind up my work at Hislop, prepare my report for
the State Department, grade the final papers, confer on the
granting of certificates and diplomas, and prepare to return to
the U.S. and Syracuse.

After two more days of delirium, I was urged by Dr. Peggy
to leave Nagpur as soon as possible for a moderate climate.
"Kashmir," she suggested. "And get a houseboat."

Professor Ehrensperger was willing to carry on with what I
could not do while away. I took with me my materials for the
final report as well as the test papers. My work on books was no
problem. I was by then near the end of the text on Indian
journalism. And I was moving along well with *Face to Face
with India*, the Friendship Press book. Four weeks later, despite
my illness, I had completed all grading and other Hislop work
and also written several articles. My Fulbright report was
finished. A small portable Olivetti typewriter stood up to it all.
Somehow I also managed to finish checking the proofs of

Journalism in Modern India and mailed them to my publisher in Bombay.

I arranged with P. D. Tandon to be my literary agent and opened a checking account with the State Bank of India. For the next 20 years, I sent him articles for Indian newspapers and magazines. They were about various topics in the USA and were intended to help bring about greater understanding of my country in India. We shared evenly the few rupees paid—when there was a return.

When we collaborated on books, Tandon sent me his impressions and reports from interviews and also the results of specific research I requested. He mailed me books and articles unattainable in the USA. Like me, he squirrels away information and has extensive files, including photographs. I, on the other hand, scoured the literature in the U.S. I wrote chapters, sending drafts to him for correction; his chapters came to me for similar treatment. He handled business arrangements with publishers, such as seeing that contracts were sent to me. He checked proofs, offered promotion plans, and other such details. We concurred on royalty arrangements by dividing evenly.

Mrs. Wolseley and I, now accompanied by my mother, who had come some months before, decided to make the medical retreat to Kashmir and the famous gardens of Srinagar as part of our return to the USA. Our original plan had been to continue around the world, going by ship from India to Australia and then via another vessel across the Pacific. But that was not the time of year for a sunstroke victim to be in the South Pacific. So we arranged bookings from Bombay to Naples and on across Europe by land and then to Liverpool in the U.K. We left Nagpur for Kashmir via Bombay and New Delhi.

The last page of my diary about the stay in India records, on sailing day, May 16, 1953: "Farewell to India. For the most part we are glad. An unusual and profitable (intellectually and spiritually) time was spent. This now comes, at least physically, to a close."

Over a month later we arrived back in Syracuse with our staggering collection of baggage.

8   **Writers in Progress**

Building the journalism school.
Writing for love—and money.
Observations on writers' conferences.
Training versus education in the
teaching of writing.

The year following my return from India saw me busy not only with normal academic work at Syracuse, but also with requests from churches and others to speak on India's social problems, religious life, press, and the launching of a journalism department there. My wife and I maintained membership in our church in Evanston, though we became affiliate members of Erwin Methodist Church in Syracuse. I served on area-wide Methodist church committees and as adviser on public relations matters to the bishop. My work was with a skilled religion writer and publicist, Carlton J. Frazier, who was in charge of the day-to-day job of preparing news releases, arranging press conferences, and other work to gain understanding of the church and its aims.[1]

My primary attention, however, went to the university's magazine department, which had been kept at full strength by

---

1. Like G. Elson Ruff, *The Lutheran's* editor; Paul Hutchinson, editor of the *Christian Century*; and Ralph Stoody, who headed the Methodist denomination's public information offices for years, Frazier was respected by press people, whether in print or electronic journalism. All these religion journalists are now gone, but they set standards for others.

Dr. Robert Root, my replacement. It began to attract more students and soon led the School of Journalism in enrollment. (It continued to do so until the late 1960s.) Those who completed the work spread the word. The growth also was part of the steady enrollment rise in the university in general and the School of Journalism in particular.

The school in 1953 and for some years later still was print oriented; it was not for another dozen years that telecommunications became an integral part of it and eventually dominated the enrollment numerically. This was a reflection of the rise in popularity of television.

Other departments grew as well, enriching the programs all the more because more electives were available. I took back not only the religion journalism courses but also critical writing, foreign press, a seminar in magazine research, and the large beginning class on the magazine field in general. Dr. Root remained on the faculty after my return and began developing a

We present Henry R. Luce (center) with a Newhouse Medal, honoring him for his dramatic success as a magazine publisher of Time, Life, *and other magazines and books. At right is Dean Wesley C. Clark. Photo by Jon Bird.*

specialty of his own—a government-financed mental health information program leading to a master's degree.[2]

Besides our work in the magazine department, both Dr. Root and I provided consulting help to editors and publishers within the print industry. Individual publishers engaged journalism teachers to critique their publications. When the school, under Dean Wesley C. Clark, formed its Mass Communication Research Center for service to any type of publication, several of us on the faculty accepted assignments to evaluate as a team. One handled graphics, another editorial practices, someone else management. In some instances the publication was near enough Syracuse to be visited by a team. Reader interest, readability, and legibility research was done under these contracts and the fees split between individuals and school.

Related to these efforts were workshops or training sessions conducted on the premises of the publications or at gatherings of staff members elsewhere, as at hotels or university conference centers. These usually covered from two days to a week of intensive work. Such activities were useful to the publications staffs and also enabled the university and the school to provide practical help to the publishing industry.

The many talents of Robert Root

It is worth pausing here to take note of Robert Root, a religion journalist of unusual background and experience who worked in tandem with me for so many years at Syracuse. He began his career at Columbia University's School of Journalism in 1936, during which time he moonlighted for the *New York Times* by covering Sunday morning services. He was paid $5 for each story.

After a year in Europe on a Pulitzer scholarship, he worked in his native state of Iowa on the *Des Moines Tribune* and its sister daily, the *Des Moines Register*, becoming an editorial writer for both papers. During World War II, he worked for the World Council of Churches in Europe, writing material for the church press and also as Geneva correspondent for the *Christian Century* magazine. When his WCC assignment ended, he free-

2. This curriculum prepared people to handle the public relations work of mental hospitals and lasted until federal support was withdrawn a decade later. By then it was being carried on by the assistant dean, Professor Burton W. Marvin, who, on my complete retirement in 1972 from Syracuse, carried on the religion journalism courses.

lanced for a year in the Near East and Asia and also was a special correspondent for the *Christian Science Monitor*, a leading international daily published by a religious denomination. He sold articles to *Newsweek* and religious publications as well. He became executive editor of Worldover Press, a news syndicate, when he returned to the States, and also taught journalism at the University of Bridgeport. After his productive years at Syracuse, he moved to Eisenhower College, where he planned a journalism program and headed world affairs studies.

Robert Root's life is an example of how religious zeal, journalistic talent, and teaching ability can be combined.

Writing for love—and money

During the consulting as well as academic work, my book and article writing continued on schedule.[3] As examples of articles I wrote for the Indian or American press, I note a few titles: "Garrison—An American Forerunner of Gandhi," *Swatantra Magazine*, Madras; "The Influence of the Religious Press," *Religion in Life*; "An American Looks at Diwali," the *Onlooker* magazine, Bombay; "Plan for Plagiarists," *The Saturday Review*; "The U.S. Election Scene," *Illustrated Weekly of India*, Bombay.

By now some reading these lists, aware that I have written many books and articles, served as consultant to publishers, and taught at writers' conferences, must think that I need several banks to hold all my earnings. Not so. One account handles them easily.

Writing, especially novels, short stories, poetry, articles, and general nonfiction books, is a notoriously underpaid occupation. For the amount of energy expended and expenses incurred, it is almost an activity a writer pays to engage in.

It is common for an article writer, for example, to devote 10 hours to gathering information from various sources and in various ways. Additional hours go into writing several drafts, taking photographs or procuring them from others, processing

3. *Journalism in Modern India* came out in 1953, the year I returned from India. *Face to Face with India* appeared in 1954. The next year saw publication of the first edition of *Careers in Religious Journalism* (New York: Association Press). The intent of this book was to help persons of any age realize the various opportunities, especially in those days, to put journalistic skills to work for the world of religion. A Hindi edition of *Journalism in Modern India* was published in 1954 by Janamanda Press in India under the title *The Art of Indian Journalism*.

them, and handling mailing costs both ways. The writer may be paid $150 or $200. That comes to about $10 to $15 an hour. From this check must be deducted expenses and taxes. Only established writers can demand travel and other expenses. (See "Why Freelancing Is Such Hard Work" in appendix 1.)

Writers on salary to newspapers and magazines fare better than free-lancers, for they have a predictable income. But their returns do not measure up to those of doctors or lawyers and might not be as high as they are if it were not for such organizations as the Newspaper Guild.

Writers on religion or writers who are religious but deal with many subjects are accustomed to doing their work with a higher motive than commerce. To many, giving away manuscripts to religious publications is a genuine sacrifice. But the earnest perform this type of stewardship, especially if the magazines and papers could not exist without such cooperation from writers. (They do, however, point out that the printers, the postal clerks, and sometimes the publishers are not asked to make a similar sacrifice.) Religion writers, furthermore, are moved to give at least part of their earnings to the causes in which they believe—their church, denominational agencies, or missionary enterprises. Perhaps, in the end, they have certain satisfactions from their work not granted those who believe the cynical sentence attributed to Samuel Johnson: "No man but a blockhead ever wrote except for money."[4]

Writers' conferences—are they worth it?

Those who write for money, for the love of writing, or for a chance to serve others through authorship have been eager to assemble, to talk shop, and exchange experiences. This urge was realized by the administration of the School of Journalism at Syracuse. It supported my proposals and those of Robert Root that we offer both general and religious writers' conferences in summer or fall.

I brought to the idea my own experiences as a faculty member of that kind of conference at Northwestern University. There were also my experiences at the Southern Baptist Convention assembly grounds in Ridgecrest, North Carolina, similar American Baptist Convention sessions in Philadelphia and

4. See "Religious Writers are Blockheads" in appendix 1.

later at the denomination's assembly grounds at Green Lake, Wisconsin.

In the 1980s, writers and editors in the USA have scores of such writers' conferences available every year.[5] Never ceasing are the debates about whether they are worth the time and expense.

Depending upon the needs of the persons considering attending, the quality of the teaching staff, the scene of the work offered, the theology dominating the conference, and the location, such sessions can be helpful or useless.

Would-be participants should study the announcements carefully and, as one would with travel folders, take them not too literally. One should calculate not only the registration fees but also the cost of travel involved, the reputation of the faculty, the activities of the organizers, and the subjects covered. Also, friends who have attended certain conferences might provide helpful evaluation.

The mechanism of these workshops for writers is essentially simple and, at least among the well managed, remarkably effective. Most of their directors and committees select an area of writing to be covered. This field is broken into subtopics, which then comprise the classes to be taught. Thus it is common to see such groups offering classes in article, novel, short story, poetry, drama, religion or secular writing, or both.

Within these categories or running alongside them are classes in style or categories based upon subject matter, such as science writing, medical writing, or business writing. Within the novel may be the novel of romance, the historical novel, novels of science fiction, novels for children, and the social problems story.

When and where to hold the conference must be arranged. Summer sessions or intersessions at colleges and universities are popular times and places, for then food and lodging are available. Practicing writers or teachers of writing or the two in one must be engaged to fill the various teaching slots. A planning committee is needed to see to it that provisions are made for entertainment, publicity, printing and advertising, and

---

5. For a list of conferences see the spring issues of *The Writer* and *Writer's Digest* magazine; readers interested especially in religion writers' conferences will find them listed in a book by William H. Gentz: *The Religious Writers Marketplace* (Philadelphia: Running Press).

other background tasks.

Although I have been on the managerial side of such conferences, it is as a faculty member that I feel most at home. I like to talk shop, but do not wish to worry about the tricks of the sound system or whether someone's mail has arrived from home. I found the transfer from my regular academic duties satisfying. But of course it never is an exact transfer, for conference and workshop class members bring somewhat different backgrounds than do students of college age.

My students in these special programs all have been adults of middle years or older, mainly women, of wide range of talent and background in the writing world, from total neophytes to well-published writers. I could not use my usual class outlines with such a group. In fact, the range of skill sometimes is the weakness of a writers' conference. Unless the sponsoring agency has considerable money, it cannot divide the novice from the experienced by having two to four sections of all major subjects in a carefully graded curriculum.

One way out of this dilemma is to have a postconference session of one or two weeks of individual training for the more capable persons enrolled. Not all will have the time or money for such personalized guidance, but sometimes a small group produces better results than large classes of writers with unlike backgrounds and quality in skills.

Thirteen summers at Green Lake

Perhaps the most satisfactory and fruitful experiences I have had came from 13 summer conferences at Green Lake, Wisconsin, site of the American Baptist Assembly grounds. It is a 1,000-acre area of natural beauty and efficient organization. Many activities occur simultaneously. Here I came to know writers on religion producing various kinds of fiction and nonfiction, including novels, short stories, and curriculum materials.

One of these was Julie McDonald who appeared in my article writing workshop in the late 1950s. Such summer training was eagerly accepted by this young woman, an Iowan of Danish descent. She not only returned to Green Lake several times but also enrolled at writers' conferences of a more literary nature at the University of Iowa.

She found jobs writing for Iowa newspapers as either

staffer or free-lancer, all the while keeping house and rearing her family and assisting her lawyer husband. She continued to write, eventually turning to fiction, mainly regional novels about the Scandinavians who settled in the Middle West. *The Sailing Out*, the last of a trilogy was published in 1982. Before that had come *Amalie's Story* and *Petra*. She also has published a children's book, a biography, a regional history, and a Danish cookbook.

One development at Green Lake always will make those sessions exceptional, even though the plan did not long remain the success hoped for by its originators. That was a miniature MacDowell Colony for religion writers. The model for this activity exists in Peterborough, New Hampshire. A retreat for

One of the most professional of my Christian writers' conference students at the American Baptist Assembly in Green Lake, Wisconsin, was Major Margaret Troutt of the Salvation Army. Russell Brandt Photo.

writers, artists, and composers, it was founded by Mrs. Arthur E. MacDowell in honor of her composer husband in what was the MacDowell summer home.

The Green Lake adaptation was the dream of the late Dr. Benjamin P. Browne, an outstanding pastor, religious educator, writer, and editor who served for a time as president of the American Baptists. He edited *Baptist Leader* magazine and was executive director of Christian Publications of the denomination.[6] Ben Browne realized that a week-long conference could not go into depth in its course offerings. He wanted a facility that could house the students, at low cost, with a writers' library, a lounge, classrooms, and bedrooms. It took several years to raise the money, but finally what became known as the National Christian Writing Center was opened and dedicated. It was a former private home near the lake and within walking distance of the dining hall and Roger Williams Inn, the conference hotel.

Postconference special classes were held in it, and some students and faculty roomed there for a week or more. At other times writers arranged to stay for varying periods to work on book and other manuscripts. But not enough individuals and organizations made use of the house to cover the costs of operating and maintaining it. Also, in bad weather, going to and from the dining hall was a problem. In winter the center often stood idle. Finally it was used for other assembly purposes.

During its short life, it was a haven for writers on religion, for it gave them opportunity to do uninterrupted work in an idyllic setting. It also encouraged fellowship among the writers who occupied the center. Although I never used it to do work of my own, I remember well, during the postconference meetings and classes in it, the lively discussions of various literary and journalistic problems.

The question we all ask

One of the unending discussions there and in the worlds of writing and education is whether people can be taught to write.

6. Books carrying the texts of Benjamin Browne's presentations at many of the Green Lake conferences include *The Writer's Conference Comes to You*, *Christian Journalism for Today*, and *The Techniques of Christian Writing*, all published by Judson Press, Philadelphia.

Rare is the textbook on writing that does not try to settle the point. I concluded long ago that certain kinds of writing can indeed be taught and have been for years. That includes most journalistic forms and a good deal of general writing that more or less depends upon formulas.

Aside from that, all a teacher can do is bring out of the nascent writer any natural skills possessed and guide the writer away from common mistakes in technique. An instructor cannot endow a student with imagination, sensitivity, and curiosity, three important requirements for effective writers. Especially are they important for someone planning a writing career.

One can read about writing and attain a little success. But if one writes under supervision and realistic conditions, much can be learned about what is now called the best hands-on practices. Workshops try to reproduce the conditions under which writers actually will do their work. Reading is important, but putting the lessons into practice in a simulated realistic situation goes much further and gives the learner enthusiasm and the test of at least semireality.

Courses I have been engaged to teach at workshops include my specialties as a university professor: magazine article writing, news and feature writing, religion journalism, church publicity, newspaper editing, book reviewing, and such general topics as research, style, and free-lancing as an occupation. But my principal workshop subject in various conferences has been magazine and newspaper article writing, as distinguished from news reports and other spot assignments.

If there is time, I not only help new writers learn to construct the parts of an article but also tackle in-depth subjects. Class members are encouraged to go on with a particular writing project after the end of a workshop by allowing extra time at home.

A substantial article can be written in a short time if a writer is near all the sources and can devote all of his or her time to the assignment, say two to four weeks. But if the writer must travel for information, take photographs and have them processed, query editors in search of an interested one, carry out research plans, develop the idea, prepare an outline, write several drafts, and organize the collected data, two months may pass before the job is done.

Most workshop students, young people as well as adults, have other demands, such as holding full-time jobs or running a household. Taking this into consideration, my arrangement is for someone in a week-long workshop, say, to be expected to submit several possible article ideas, with a report on the market possibilities and on what sources can be foreseen at the time. A sample query letter also is assigned.

The writer then has a month after returning home to submit the best possible draft. I critique this and suggest further research or other work still needed. Time then is allowed for the revision. The old and new manuscripts then are returned to me and the process is repeated if necessary. Pictures and other illustrations are submitted either with the first or second versions.

I never have counted and no longer have records to allow me to count, but I know that some of these articles have been published, mainly in the religion press. On the other hand, other writers never went beyond the conference or workshop session. Still others lost interest in submitting their material when a second or third draft was requested. And some fell out of the system after a few editors turned down the scripts.

How does one help new writers to be effective in putting one word after another on paper or a screen? That part of the training can be accomplished by asking writers to produce short pieces at first. These bits might be for possible publication as fillers or brief units of departments or columns. These I edit closely, return, and request improved versions the next session, along with the originals, so I can check what has been done.

What I red-pencil is the usual set of faults in the preprofessionals' work (not that professionals are always free of flaws): misspellings, faulty grammar, tautology, misusages, verbosity, illogical construction, redundancy, and factual inaccuracies. This procedure is not confined to workshops in religion conferences or classes but also appears in secular meetings in which I take part.

I find that new writers always are grateful for vigorous red-penciling. There no doubt are those who, in reality, consider me a nitpicker. But I stand behind my methods because I not only pick nits but also dwell on the construction of the piece of writing, its focus and purpose, and other larger considerations that a dictionary and a style manual cannot correct.

Education versus training—some choices

One of the issues that American universities, colleges, and media industries have to face is how standard, full-length education compares to the shorter workshop training programs. In a nation like the USA, with its many advanced professional occupations—medicine, law, communications, education, the sciences, and the arts with their numerous subdivisions— education in-depth, technological or general, is by far the more effective.

But for quick results in practical areas, short-term, workshop programs in writing, editing, and design, to name a few, have been found more feasible. This is usually in countries where advanced skills and abilities cannot be so advantageously used and where equipment and public receptivity are not at the point where in-depth study is needed. Yet this general view needs to be adjusted to the areas of the world that are more or less developed in some activity. Staying with communications further: workshops are unquestionably more useful to the media in Burma, say, than long-term graduate education as offered in the United Kingdom or Germany.

Both types of training are valuable, then, and both will not necessarily be needed in any one area or early in any campaign to be of help. It is not so much which but when the nation or community is ready for either.

What about respective long-term effects? Results from writers' workshops are the most difficult to measure because in most cases no records at all are kept on the whereabouts of past students. Yet even here, as in the case of Julie McDonald, it is possible to keep in touch with their progress.

As for my own graduate students, I have indicated elsewhere that certain of them have benefited from advanced training and education in the academic context. (See pp. 64-65, 113-115.) To this list could be added others. Mlle. Christine de Rivoyre, for instance, came to Syracuse from the Sorbonne in Paris and later joined the staff of *Le Monde*, one of Paris's outstanding dailies. Since then she has won national awards for her fiction. Laura Pilarski, an American of Polish descent and author of *They Came from Poland*, became a reporter for the *Milwaukee Journal* after the Syracuse course, and then a European correspondent for the McGraw-Hill News Service. Jon C. Halter became a ranking editor on the staff of *Boys' Life* magazine and later wrote successful books for boys. Omar Eby, another Syracuse graduate, was a Mennonite who taught in Somalia, Tanzania, and Zambia, as well as in the USA. Recently he joined the faculty of Eastern Mennonite College and is an author of a number of books. Robert Phillips, who went into advertising, makes a steady literary contribution through his novels, short stories, and literary criticism.

Such glimpses of former students can be multiplied several times over. But my reports on the successful ones may not be a fair test of the system of making academic preparation for journalism available. There are other students on whom I have negative reports and many more on whose careers—in communications or otherwise—I have no information whatsoever. Still, having these and other students as friends even beyond graduation has given a special purpose and continuity to my years in journalism education. They remain in memory more sharply than do the courses, the academic surroundings, the curricula.

9 Discovery of Black Journalism

A hidden journalism struggles for a voice. Research and writing on the Afro-American press.

While I was in newspaper work and journalism teaching in Illinois, I came to know an alderman in the city of Evanston named Edwin B. Jourdain. I first knew him during the days I covered city hall for the Evanston *Daily News-Index.*

Ordinarily I would make no special mention of Mr. Jourdain's race, which was black, but it is important to this chapter. For here I recount how I happened, a quarter of a century after knowing him, to teach one of the first courses in the United States on Afro-American journalism and write a book about that journalism.

As does many a politician, especially in minority groups, Mr. Jourdain established a newspaper. He wanted to communicate dependably through this weekly with his constituency in Evanston's fifth ward. The *Daily News-Index* was willing to cover the black community, difficult as it was to report such news. But it was not enough. We lacked capital and revenue to add the staff that would be needed.

Our rival, the *Evanston Review*, a weekly that looked like a magazine but was mainly news, tried to cover in one issue all of what we did in six. Thus, it provided even less news of the black community. A cheaper advertising medium than the *Daily News-Index*, it had more accounts than we did. But it was reluctant, under some of its ownerships, to distribute itself in the black community. The reason was that some merchants objected to minority citizens' patronizing their stores, especially if they were trying on women's garments. The temper of those times can be seen in a personal experience.

Ever since my freshman year at Northwestern, I have frequently written free-lance articles for business publications. Business papers and magazines then were called trade journals since they began as mouthpieces for certain trades. My articles were used, with pictures I took, in magazines of the leather, laundry, shoe manufacturing, grocery, window display, and other industries and services. Such periodicals, today as then, valued accounts of specific retail shops or small services that had become successful through economies, shortcuts and innovations in display, pricing, or some other such area.

A small Evanston cleaning and pressing firm was one such success story. Its owners and staff were all women, which was my angle, for then it was something novel. I took pictures and collected data and the piece was published. I left a copy of the issue containing the article at the shop; the owner was not in.

About two weeks later she phoned me at home.

"How could you do that to me?" she demanded, sounding both angry and grief-stricken.

I could not imagine what I had done.

"What's wrong?" I asked. "Are there mistakes in the article?"

"It's that picture," she said, now tearful. "How could you do that when I was so kind to you?"

"But I took the picture when you were there. You saw me take it. I still don't understand what the trouble is."

She hung up. I never learned from her what was wrong. At least she didn't sue for whatever it was. I studied the article and especially the photo. It showed four women at three ironing boards and one pressing machine. All were facing the camera but continuing to work. Two were black. It then dawned on me. They were black.

Perhaps the proprietor had lost business. It may have been shown to one of the women customers. Or the white women employees may have complained about being pictured working with black women. I never was able to find out.

I told my friend Alderman Jourdain about it, and he voiced the theory that only race prejudice could explain the owner's complaint. I was reminded of this incident not long ago when a friend, a man in this instance, explained why he refuses to use laundromats. He had the same reason: his clothes might be washed in machines used by different races.

In several sessions with Mr. Jourdain, I asked questions about his newspaper venture. His answers summarized the history, in brief, of black newspaper journalism in the USA. He pointed out that he could not reasonably expect the *Daily News-Index* or the *Evanston Review* to run the minutiae of the black community news and certainly not many articles or editorials supporting his campaign for reelection or advancing his plans for bettering the condition of the black residents. He was satisfied with endorsement, but he needed much more than that and thought only his paper could provide it.

He shared his problems with me. He was publishing at a loss and having trouble collecting news, although some people brought it to him whereas they hesitated to enter the *Daily News-Index* or *Review* building offices to do so. Like the owners of general newspapers, he was unable to find enough boys or men to take the paper house-to-house and collect payment for it. Having a glimpse into his problems set me to thinking about minority journalism in the USA. I had, thanks to my pastor and the church, and to Bible classes and general reading, described earlier, a measure of sympathy for these journalistic underdogs.

Research in the Afro-American press

I became specifically interested in the large Afro-American press of Chicago and other influential papers in Pittsburgh, Baltimore, and New York.

Black magazines also came in for study. *Negro Digest* by no means was the first, but it was important because it launched in Chicago a company whose owner, John H. Johnson, was to become the leading entrepreneur of black magazine journalism and television in the country. Ultimately unsuccessful, *Negro Digest* was the foundation for such highly successful periodicals as *Ebony* and *Jet*.

Johnson's story and the histories of these and other magazines he later founded became parts of my magazine and history of journalism courses at Northwestern and elsewhere. Information about black journalism was skimpy, but between the Chicago Public, Newberry, and John Crerar libraries in downtown Chicago or Near North Side, I was able to prepare a lecture. I later regretted that I did not keep even one copy of the Jourdain paper or those printed in Chicago at that time. By then my research began showing up in other publications; two articles on the future of the black press, as I could read it then, appeared in *Commonweal* and *Negro Digest*.

When I moved to Syracuse I continued adding to my store of black press information and examples. Since that city was a station on the underground in the Civil War period during which blacks went to Canada to escape persecution, I found considerably more background. I came to realize how much of a protest press the early black newspapers were, with their campaigns for integration, removal of repressive post-Reconstruction legislation, abolition of slavery, and integration. And, in a century's time, how it had turned into much more of a commercial proposition than a crusading press, forced to be that to survive at all in the highly industrialized society that America had become.

About 10 percent of Syracuse's population was black, all jammed into a neighborhood not far from the downtown store-bank-office building complex. There it was easy to find black publications, including the one long-lived weekly that served the city but was killed after the black community was broken up into small units by housing developments. The *Progressive American* no longer could function in that dispersed readership.

Little by little I assembled information, still not knowing how valuable it would be some years later. At one point I was aided by having in one of my classes the granddaughter of the founding editor, in the nineteenth century, of one of the city's earliest papers. This young woman, Letitia Harris, brought to class a tear sheet of the front page and another containing an editorial by her grandfather. Syracuse has had, with the exception of the *Progressive American*, a series of the usual newsless, opinion-dominated weeklies for many years, but no magazines. During my absence in India this research was halted and then renewed later.

A course and a text

It was not until 1968 that my interest in the black press was tapped vigorously. Governor Nelson A. Rockefeller of New York sent a memorandum to heads of all colleges and universities in the state urging them to launch programs that would aid members of the black race to learn more about their heritage. The Syracuse University administration in turn appealed to its individual schools and colleges.

Dean Clark of Newhouse shared the memorandum with the faculty and requested suggestions. Mine was to offer a course on the contemporary black press. The idea was approved by him, the faculty, and the central administration. The course was the nation's first, so far as I have been able to learn, for even the few journalism programs in black colleges did not teach much about the black press. It met in the fall of 1970 with an enrollment of 32 and continued to be offered five times in three years. White students always predominated in the class, mainly because blacks were a minority in Newhouse and nonjournalism students of any race were not admitted if they lacked the professional prerequisites.

Leading black journalists were among the outside speakers I brought for a few class lectures. One of these was Robert E. Johnson, a Syracuse journalism alumnus and editor of *Jet*, a weekly news magazine.[1] Another was George M. Daniels, a specialist on African affairs for the United Methodist Church, author of several books on Africa, a journalism graduate of Drake and Columbia universities, and a former staff member of black newspapers and white religious magazines.

Aware of the great lack of general literature on black journalism, I soon proposed to a publishing firm that I prepare a textbook. It would be used in courses like my own, which were being established in other institutions. At first there was little interest. But as the nation began to realize the growing importance of black society in American life, the sad neglect of it in the past, and its need for greater opportunities to take its rightful and important place, the interest in learning more about black people rose.

---

1. Today Robert E. Johnson is vice president and associate publisher of the highly successful Johnson Publishing Company in Chicago (although he is not related to John H. Johnson, the publisher).

The Iowa State University Press, which already had published my *Understanding Magazines*, agreed to examine sample chapters and an outline. *The Black Press, U.S.A.* was published in time for use during the third offering of the course.[2] Its architecture followed in general the pattern of the Syracuse course, which was a survey covering characteristics, briefly reporting the history of black publications down to the early 1970s, analyzing content of newspapers and magazines, noting vocational problems of the black journalist on black and white papers and other media, describing basic operations, competition, and weaknesses and strengths. It ended with a forecast of the eventual disappearance of this press resulting possibly from the amalgamation of the races through mutual acceptance.[3]

During the years that Syracuse offered the course, my outline was requested by other teachers, and the book became the text for similar courses at both white and black colleges and universities. At this writing, *The Black Press, U.S.A.* still is in print, but needs updating.

Class members went to work in the black or white press. Two of the black students, both women, now are on the *Newsweek* magazine staff; one joined it after being a writer for the New York *Amsterdam News*, a large black weekly, and for *Essence*, the leading magazine for black women.

Both course and book helped me to be useful in arousing interest in this minority press. In fact, just as India fixed in me an unceasing interest in that country that has lasted three decades thus far, so the black press course and the articles and books developing from it nurtured my absorption in that extraordinary journalism.[4]

The black press—a definition

Also produced by the course and book were inquiries from people puzzled about how a medium of communication can be classified by race. What, they asked, determines it? This problem was faced at the outset of the Syracuse course. To our

2. Roland E. Wolseley, *The Black Press U.S.A.* (Ames, Iowa: Iowa State University Press, 1971). A revised second printing came out in 1972.
3. By 1985 part of this forecast was proving to be correct, for the black newspaper in particular was going into decline.
4. Other authors and scholars took up this study. See, for instance, Henry G. La Brie III, *Perspectives of the Black Press, 1974* (Kennebunkport, Maine: Mercer House Press, 1974); also, *A Survey of Black Newspapers in America* (Mercer House, 1979).

satisfaction, at least, it was settled and some other scholars have accepted it.

A black publication, it was concluded, is one under these conditions: black persons own and manage it; the publication must be intended for black consumers; it must "serve, speak and fight for the black minority." Whites are not excluded from participating, but should not be in control.

Placed against the history of the black press's struggle to survive, this definition is realistic. During their existence in the USA, beginning in 1827 with the New York weekly, *Freedom's Journal*, the black publications (and later black radio and television) for the most part have met the conditions. White money, as it might be put, has kept some alive that would have died otherwise. The enterprise that succeeds today is the exception. Most of the media are small; even blacks themselves often are unaware of them.

Take, for example, the college-educated businessman I was talking to one day. In illustrating the shortcomings of the white-owned press, I mentioned the existence of the black press as an attempt to compensate for those shortcomings. I named the two black newspapers in the community. He had never heard of either nor was he aware of the black press in general.

"I didn't know that blacks have their own publications," he said. "Why do they need them? Aren't the white papers good enough for them?"

"They read the white papers, of course," I replied. "But they also generate a lot of news that is overlooked by the white press. Ten percent of this city's population is black. That's about 18,000 people. How much news of these people do you see in our two white-owned dailies?"

He could remember only crime stories. I mentioned other occasional stories: a wedding now and then, or an obituary. I pointed out that most of the routine news is not covered.

"Such as what?"

"Public meetings, church services, openings of new businesses, engagements, weddings, funerals, sports."

I then showed him my black press books and others on that press. He was amazed at the extent, diversity, and problems.

When I told him that American Indians also have their publications, he once more was astonished. (He would not have known what I meant had I called them by what they prefer,

Native Americans.) He never had even wondered, he said, if they had a press.[5]

The hidden journalism

But he could not be blamed for being unaware of these special presses. They might be called a secret or hidden journalism. Few of these papers and magazines are in city libraries; if they are, they usually are put into shelving reserved for free copies provided by proponents of some minority, frequently religious bodies outside the mainstream. No more than a few— and those either black or Hispanic only—are on newsstands except in areas of the country with large black, Native American, or other minority populations.

The problems faced by the black media are almost the same for the other minority presses. But for these, the problems sometimes are even more severe because their audiences are even smaller and their constituents are more isolated in the society or too widely dispersed through the nation.

As the national interest in black studies dropped and students became more conventional in their views and aims, the black press course at Syracuse drew only a handful. It continued only until my retirement in mid-1972. By 1973 it still was in the Newhouse course catalog, but never was offered again. In two more years it was eliminated from the literature and buried in the vast graveyard of courses that for one reason or another have lost student or administrative support.[6]

5. See James E. Murphy and Sharon M. Murphy. *Let My People Know: American Indian Journalism*. Norman: Oklahoma University Press, 1981.
6. I always shall be grateful to the university administration, especially to Dean Wesley C. Clark of the Newhouse School, for the support he gave to this pioneering program. I also received encouragement from other faculty members, notably Dr. Robert Root, whose views on the race question paralleled my own so closely.

10 Teaching Ends, Writing Continues

Late sixties. Time of questioning values. Students in print. Of making many books. Travel writing.

A new experience for U.S. teachers and students alike brightened the late sixties, the last years of my university service. This was an apparent show of social conscience by a large segment of the student body and faculty.

The violence was largely against such inanimate objects as campus gateways, doors, and varieties of rubbish that could be stacked. Much as I deplored such use of force, I respected the convictions of students and a few teachers who were honestly rebellious and not vandals. I was cheered because I knew that many of the students, some of them my own, and even some of the staid professors, were thinking of someone other than themselves.

They were becoming disturbed by an all-too-ready resort to war, particularly America's military policy in Southeast Asia. They also were upset by discrimination against women and racial or religious minorities and by the abuses of the environment. Students known as the flower children came from this generation of protestors.

Some of the tricks played—locking administrators in their offices or smearing paint on walls and doors—were childish.

One might expect nothing better from partially educated young persons, but did not expect graduate students at work on doctorates or junior faculty members to act as some did.

But we must remember that they were not, like so many students before them and in the 1980s, willing to accept the status quo. Granted, some were unrealistic, some intolerant, and many self-indulgent, but at least they were seeking creative alternatives for living and for solving problems. For better or for worse, something was happening in their heads. That, after all, is a function of a university education: to stimulate thinking.

Some of my colleagues were disturbed by the generally grubby look of these rebels. They often were grubby indeed: barefooted, long-haired, clothed in garments apparently never washed. But I found that most I knew personally were idealists and often among the brainier and more original members of my classes, with questioning minds that belong in a university.

Perhaps I viewed what went on as a social phenomenon whose aims, if not whose methods, I could approve because it did not touch me closely. A few students in the professional schools (law, journalism, medicine, business) took part in the ructions but most were too serious-minded and too worried about their job-getting chances to risk on their records such revolutionary activity as piling logs against gates or leading protest meetings. Attendance was lowered in my classes but none were dismissed. Little was done to the Newhouse building. Graffiti appeared on the outside walls, mostly referring to Vietnam, condemning U.S. involvement in that country.

A good many of these young people with whom I have kept in touch have lost most of their social zeal and become corporation men and women. They measure success by material progress. Yet some are like the girl who always wore big picture hats to class. She defied tradition. Stocking caps to protect against the winter storms, yes. But no coed then or now would wear a dressy hat to class.

She defied other traditions later, took part in political rallies, then ran for city common council and won with her big hat on; next she married and had a child, and at this writing is in the state legislature as a spur in the backs of the conservatives.

Others stood for social progress in their own ways, albeit more calmly than in the unrestful period of their last years in the university. I recall also, on the other hand, the crusader who, on getting his advertising degree, immediately dressed like the inhabitants of advertising agency offices on Madison Avenue in New York City: neat, dark suit, matching shoes and socks, even a felt hat to coordinate with his topcoat.

Survival and "me first"

The need to survive in Western society explains the falling away of the idealists. A good many people of the idealists' generation grew up with the philosophy that personal progress must be measured in terms of money and objects owned. This originated with the generations that saw the industrialization of the West. By the middle of the twentieth century, a college education became necessary for success in business and the professions. Students often came chiefly to prepare themselves for an occupation, preferably a highly paid one. "Me first" became the overwhelming motive for learning.

As an example, for many years I began the first class sessions of my courses with an attempt to become familiar with each student's background and their motives for taking the class. The latter inquiry was answered anonymously. Either the students were shy about admitting to idealistic motives or were, as I said, concerned largely with self-advancement, fame, and high salary.

Particularly was this true of athletes, who considered a university preparation for a career on the gridiron, the ball field, or the basketball court. They did not necessarily come for the sake of knowledge and wisdom, to stretch their minds with new ideas, facts, and concepts, nor to develop their talents with the idea of serving society before serving themselves.

Nor were faculty members vastly more socially minded than students, as one can learn by serving on committees and playing tennis with colleagues. They, too, were the products of mixed motives. They did not, therefore, choose to contest the falseness of the "me first" motivation in earning a college education. On the contrary. The lack of unity among faculties in Western nations is commonplace. "Me first" is an academic slogan, also.

I came up against this mentality during all my teaching and in a variety of ways. I fought it in the classroom whether it was in Evanston, Syracuse, Nagpur, or in universities where I did short stints. Jacques Ellul, the French philosopher, educator, and churchman, has been critical of places that "turn out good little technicians who will make capable executives but nonentities." My conviction was that the more educational institutions become like that, the less place there is for selflessness. It is at this point incidentally that the church-related college plays an important part and why the religious writers' conference is more socially useful than the secular conference, which in my experience often is led by persons with little respect for the Christian religion and its concern for the welfare of people in general.

In secular universities, faculty take little part in campus religious activity. Some do not, of course, because they belong to churches in the community. But these have been in no large numbers, if my associates are a fair sampling, wherever I have taught, except in India. There I was on the faculty of a Christian college within a secular university. The university faculty was composed of many Hindus and Muslims as well as members of Jain and other sects. And religious persons in India and other Southeast Asian countries generally allow their beliefs to permeate their lives far more than do Christians of the West. Furthermore, those in the West who are not Christian generally see no merit in the selflessness of true religion. People who are altruistic, they say cynically, really are selfish.

Once, for example, when teaching the course in black journalism at Syracuse, I invited a black professor of anthropology to speak to the class about his views on the press of his racial group in the USA, what use he made of it, and especially his opinions of its scholarly journals. In the course of the discussion, the black students, a few of whom were willing to work for less money on the minority press in order to help strengthen that press, were accused by him of being essentially selfish.

"There is no such thing as altruism," he insisted. "We all do good things to gratify ourselves. We are really just trying to cover up our selfish purposes by appearing to do something for others." The discussion then nearly got out of hand because some of the whites and blacks were so upset by what they considered a cynical view.

At no time in my teaching career did I accept the argument the anthropologist had championed, one that also can be heard as readily in classes in psychology and sociology at secular colleges. On the contrary, I have admitted that we all must give self-advancement a respectable place in our list of aims merely to survive in our materialistic society. But I put above it doing what we can for others, not in the expectation of doing good and being rewarded for it, but that, being ourselves, we cannot do otherwise.

Students in print

In many cases, this view is exemplified in my students. I enjoy reflecting on them and their careers because after 11 years at Northwestern and 26 at Syracuse as well as time spent teaching at other colleges, I have acquired among them many friends. These friends not only write letters but also keep me informed about their social involvement and book writing, often sending me autographed copies. When they do not and I am particularly interested in the book, I instruct my alter ego, Fred Welch (my initials lurk in his name), to buy it for me for Christmas or my birthday.

These books are kept in separate racks in my downstairs library. (For a partial list see appendix 2.) They are by no means the full output of former students. Some have written but not reported the fact to me, and I somehow have failed to see reviews, especially if they are general books or highly specialized ones not in any of my fields of interest. Whether or not on this list, any number of my students could be subjects for vignettes.

While still in his thirties and less than a decade after his graduation from Newhouse, Ronald Patterson, for example, became editor in chief of Abingdon Press, one of the most prestigious positions in U.S. religion publishing. Another, John Lovelace, after founding a religion journalism program at Oklahoma Baptist University in Shawnee, became managing editor of the *United Methodist Reporter*. Mary Hamilton became an instructor in journalism at St. Bonaventure University in New York. James P. Colligan is now photojournalist for the National Catholic News Service in Tokyo, Japan; his byline appears in leading Catholic periodicals, including *Catholic Digest, Maryknoll*, and the *Sign*. Barbara Love, former candidate for the U.S. Olympic swim team, has become executive editor of *Folio*, a magazine devoted to the U.S. magazine industry.

Two other students, both women from outside the country,

complete this brief galley of students in print.

One of the magazine department advisees at Syracuse who reported for counseling in the later 1960s was a girl who looked Spanish—dark eyes and hair and the name Claudia Caruana. I was so sure that she was of that background that when she sat down beside my desk I said, "Usted habla Español?"

"No," she said. "I'm not Spanish. Or even Latin American."

"So, then where are you from?" There was one clue in her speech; she had said New Yawk.

"Malta. My mother and father are from there."

I could not remember ever having had someone of Maltese descent in a class or having known anyone from those islands. The encounter aroused my interest in the little Mediterranean republic. In 1978 and 1979 I visited Malta and later published articles about it. In fact, I became so interested in its history, its unusual population, and its severe political and social problems, I planned a book on it. But it never went past the planning and proposal stages; too limited an audience, the publishers said. Claudia helped me with source material. We have corresponded ever since.

Miss Caruana proceeded through the magazine sequence, and has been in magazine editorial work for a decade so far, chiefly as associate editor of *Chemical Engineering Progress* magazine. But she also is a busy free-lancer, contributing articles and short stories to religious, food, consumer, journalism, and other periodicals, editing books for several publishers, and teaching journalism at two universities.

A sketch of an entirely different sort of biography is that of Mrs. Radhakrishna Rao of Hyderabad, India. That was not her name while she was at Syracuse. She was Devikarani Satyanarayana, a dainty young woman who was a frequent subject for photographs taken by students in the department of that art.

Her aim was to learn American magazine techniques so she could write or edit for periodicals in the USA. She obtained her master's degree in magazine journalism, returned to India to visit her family, and at the strong urging of her father, flew back to Syracuse to start work on a Ph.D. in mass communications, still emphasizing the magazine field.

She completed most of the course work but lost interest

when she could not settle on a dissertation topic suitable to both her and the graduate division faculty of Newhouse. Leaving the university, she worked for a time for a pharmaceutical firm in Norwich, New York as a special writer of materials to appear in specialized magazines. Then she returned to India, without her doctor's degree.

She became an instructor in journalism in the department of that subject at Osmania University in Hyderabad. Some years later she married a noted Indian surgeon who had practiced for 15 years in the United Kingdom and, at the time of their wedding, had an important practice in Hyderabad.

When she wrote me about her marriage she said: "I got my doctor, after all."

Publisher jumping

During the decade of the sixties, my own writing went on at the usual pace. Old books were revised and republished. One, *Newsmen at Work*, prepared with Laurence R. Campbell, and published in 1949, was completely rewritten for a different publisher and brought out under a new title, *How to Report and Write the News*.[1] It was only moderately successful in sales, however, partly because of an onrush of competing texts and the dominance of one book written by my old friend from the Evanston *Daily News-Index* and Medill School of Journalism days, Curtis D. MacDougall. His *Interpretative Reporting* has ruled the field for a half century.

How to Report and Write the News was the result of an activity in the book world not often described: jumping, or shifting, from one publisher to another. These occur for several reasons. Market analysis being a not entirely scientific business, a publisher cannot be sure of the demand for a certain title. In college textbooks there usually is more knowledge of the potential. The number of courses in which a book might be used as a first text or as auxiliary reading offers a clue. But the decision may be against the author even so if the field is crowded with competing volumes and the potential sale is not expected to be sufficient to offset the cost of promotion and of manufacturing the revised book.

---

1. Laurence R. Campbell and Roland E. Wolseley, *How to Report and Write the News* (Englewood Cliffs, N.J.: Prentice-Hall, 1961).

One problem that arises in such shifts, aside from the business matter of an equal if not improved publishing agreement, is retaining the facts from the first version without repeating too closely the style and handling of those facts. It requires careful rephrasing as well as resisting the temptation to pick up whole pages unchanged. Another is keeping the book useful to teachers accustomed to the structure of the original version. Too much change means that instructors must recast their notes. That is one explanation of why old, outdated books continue to sell beyond their normal life span.

A query, then Holland

Having already written a book on a foreign country—India—I decided about this time to try another. This one, on Holland, originated in an entirely different way.[2]

A fellow member of the faculty at Green Lake Christian Writers' Conference in Wisconsin in the mid-1960s was Charles Paul May, author of two books for Thomas Nelson in its World Neighbors Series. One was on Central America, the other on Chile. At the time he was working on another, covering Peru, Bolivia, and Ecuador. We discussed his working methods. He let me see his publishing agreement. Reading the back list of the series, I noticed that Holland, Belgium, and Luxembourg were not included.

Since I had visited all three already, Holland several times, I queried the series editor, enclosing a proposed outline and mention of my book on India. After an exchange of letters, I received an agreement and immediately planned another European trip in the interest of the new book.

Various kinds of preparations were made. For instance, I notified certain foreign agencies with offices in the United States of my forthcoming trip and its purpose. They alerted their central offices at home. I also wrote airlines, here and overseas, about my plans, requesting aerial views, since I do not take such photographs.

I received all the cooperation I could ask. Special photographs were taken for the book in Holland; I had my choice of hundreds of still prints from all three countries. I was introduced to people in each in all walks of life: students, householders,

---

2. Roland E. Wolseley, *The Low Countries: Gateways to Europe* (Camden, N.J.: Thomas Nelson, 1969).

professional men and women, factory workers; my wife and I were entertained in the homes of farmers and city clerks.

As part of my preparations, I made up a notebook in which I recorded history and current information. I also set up folders for each chapter, the front matter (title page, table of contents and the like), and illustrations. These were ready to accept the pounds of paper I brought back from the three countries and from all my other sources—books read at any time before publication; articles of any sort, notes of interviews done in the U.S. before departing for Europe, information gleaned via letters.

Moreover, I noted carefully how other authors in the series had organized their books, selected their vocabularies, and obtained illustrations. Being consistent to the form was important because the series was heavily used in schools. I was able to see many of the other books by going to the children's departments of local libraries. I particularly observed the kinds of photographs taken by the authors themselves, since I planned to submit some myself. When published, the book contained many photographs; one-fourth of them I had snapped.

New world of travel writing

The book on Holland was to be a preamble for later travel writing. Well before retirement, I reflected upon how to use my

My final class session at the School of Public Communications was of an advanced research seminar on magazines. Bill Jerome (right) was the photographer.

time when I no longer was teaching. To what social purpose could I put it? I concluded that, as before, my contribution could be through the only skill I had: writing. And along with writing there would continue the related skill of editing, and the passing along of my accumulated experience in publishing.

I did decide to make one change, however. It would be in the direction of my writing. Until the mid-1960s, I had written mainly textbooks; the exceptions were volumes on religion journalism, its career possibilities, and travel. I wanted to take advantage of being free to travel in particular. For that is one of the rewards of retirement from the pedagogical life unless one must go on earning by teaching elsewhere. I therefore decided to link travel and writing more than ever before. I particularly wanted to write more travel articles for newspapers and magazines.

My official retirement date was mid-1969. At that time a teacher at Syracuse had the option of up to three more years on full or part-time. I chose part-time, handling a lighter load and freed of administrative responsibilities. I still could not travel except in summer, but I had time to study travel writing by reading the travel sections of the larger papers received at the local libraries. I also started a file of examples of articles, for I wanted to understand the various possible types. These included stories about geographical areas, specific cities, life-styles of foreign peoples, problems and incidents of traveling, and humor. By my full retirement in 1972, I was ready to take off or mount the gangplank.

Five years later I had published one or more travel articles in the *Christian Science Monitor*, *Dallas News*, *Washington Post*, *Long Island Newsday*, *Bombay Free-Press Journal*, *Syracuse Post-Standard*, *Bombay Mirror*, *Trip & Tour*, *Home*, *Encore*, *World Book and Travel Report*, and several dozen in the church magazines, including *Reachout*, *Evangel*, and *Accent on Youth*. During the same period dozens more appeared on black press subjects in a score of other newspapers and magazines, both religious and secular.

11

All in a Day's Work

A day in the life of a writer. Writing for the general market. The writer and rejections. Bad editors—and good.

I often am asked how much time I spend writing a book or article. Or how much time is devoted to some part of the work, such as research, writing drafts, and obtaining illustrations.

I cannot answer with any hope even of approximating a figure. I do not keep records of how much time I put in on writing and I do not know any writers who do. Time and motion studies are useful in some other businesses, but in the business of writing, there are factors that may be unique with that art. They are also so time-consuming to measure that a writer's productivity would suffer.

I could not even describe a typical writing day in my life, at any stage of it, either as a full-time journalist, a full-time teacher, or a full-time free-lancer. One day, to help clear up my thinking on a problem, I will hardly work at all on a book in progress. Another day I may put in an hour on various trivia of daily existence—brushing teeth, doing dishes, mailing letters, pressing clothes—and 13 hours of more or less steady labor on a manuscript, with time out for ablutions and eating a hasty meal or two.

Another day about one or two hours each will go to book work, doing part of a magazine article, writing a book review, reading books to be reviewed, making out file cards related to a book, preparing letters pertaining to my writing or to carrying on my daily life, doing my accounts, attending to personal mail, filing clippings, searching for photographs or other illustrations, going to the library or my university office to consult materials, and drafting a proposal for a book or an article.

Throw these three kinds of days together and draw out different segments and you have still another profile of a day different from those three. The elements in my work days are like cards in a pack. Thousands of combinations are possible, and no two days are exactly alike in the use of time.

Furthermore, a writer works even while riding to a bank in the city bus or standing in line at a supermarket. Overheard conversation may ignite an idea, or the subconscious mind may solve a writing problem under any circumstances, including sleep.

The most nearly accurate answer to the question, "How much time?" is: 24 hours a day.

The elements in my work days are like cards in a pack. Thousands of combinations are possible and no two days are exactly alike.

Writing for the general market

My resolve to broaden the scope of my writing before I was fully retired involved not only subject matter but also writing techniques. I had attempted all my writing life to avoid the jargon of the academic specialist. Fortunately, teachers of journalism are less likely to be trapped in the vocabulary of a specialty because journalism has only a small glossary; in addition, it has the objective of clear communication. The only exception is the group sometimes called communicologists, that is, researchers who have developed a necessary shortcut language about communications.

Because I was aiming at a more popular or general market than the publications of communications and religion, I needed to review such details as vocabulary selection, sentence and paragraph length, use of connectives, conciseness of expression, and suitability of each topic to the readers I hoped to win.

Adjustments, I found, were necessary in each of these five areas.

Vocabulary, first of all, is much different in journalistic writing than in more formal or literary composition. Writers for scholarly magazines, such as the *Journal of Sociology*, can assume that their readers are deeply interested in their subject, well informed about it, and understand the special language usually used in the publication's pages.

But readers of general circulation newspapers and magazines do not have those attitudes or preparation for special topics. Editors and writers must struggle to interest them in many subjects that do not touch their lives closely. For this purpose, simple words are more serviceable than any other. Such catering to readers' apparent limitations, however, must be regulated, or vocabularies never will grow. Writers who want to do a little educating along the way might use a specialized term and follow it with a parenthetical explanation or definition.

Sentence and paragraph lengths also are not the same for all kinds of publications, including books. Long sentences are difficult for some readers to follow, especially if the sentences are not simply constructed. The writer of long sentences assumes that the scholar can keep his or her mind on what is being read because of intense interest in the material.

But the man or woman on the street, it must be remembered, must read under conditions that make concentration difficult. After leaving the street this reader enters subway or bus, airport terminal, or doctor's office, or in summer sits on a park bench and in winter in a cafeteria. Such readers are beset by noises: clacking dishes, background talk, the always present piped-in music, the explosions of city buses, the roaring of planes, and the stopping and starting of cars as they are governed by traffic lights.

Because of the difficulty such readers have in concentrating, paragraphs in more general publications are kept short. They may be 40 lines long in more academic books, depending upon the page size, but in newspapers and general magazines, they may run only from 5 to 10 lines.

There is another reason for such shortness. Whether the eyes are those of a scholar or a general reader, they tire quickly if the paragraph is both deep and wide. That is why newspapers and many magazines keep their columns to more or less two inches wide. Then there is the point that in newspapers, particularly, it is easier to adjust length of materials if paragraphs are short. Cuts, especially from the bottom, can then be made without seriously damaging the structure of the piece.

Connectives, sometimes called conjunctions, I had to be reminded from grammar school days, are used differently by the general writer than by the writer for specialists. I had to give more attention to my use of *nevertheless, and, but, for example, however, yes, no, yet, so, while, also* and others. These words are used less by newspaper writers than book or magazine writers. If one or more paragraphs in different parts of a newspaper piece must be removed by an editor, a conjunction can cause problems, for what is referred to by the connecting word may no longer be in the text.

Conciseness is a quality in writing to which I have aspired for years. It is vital in journalism not only to make reading easier, but because space often is at a premium. A large daily in the USA receives for publication from its staff members, independent writers, and syndicated news and other copy services four times more material than it can possibly print in a day's issue or even in several editions.

In other than Western nations, the need for conciseness is just as great, for even if the amount of material is not so abundant, the size of newspapers, to continue the example in that medium, is much smaller than in the West. Important American dailies on ordinary days may run from 40 to 60 large pages; many important cities in other continents are able to support only a few daily papers of a dozen or 16 pages, some even tabloid size.

A writer must remember, also, that conciseness can be taken to excess. It can make reading more difficult because the words are so tightly packed they cannot be understood without additional reading. Here, then, I realized, is a battle between objectives. But I had to learn it if I was to satisfy editorial and space demands as well as readers' understanding.

Making the writing suitable for readers is a matter of taking aim at the right target. A writer who is unaware that most of his or her likely readers have no understanding or concern about, let us say, steamship operation or the politics of Sri Lanka will have a difficult time gaining and holding their attention. (As a case in point, probably only one in ten would know Sri Lanka once was called Ceylon and is off the southeast tip of India.) One of the major reasons that many writers fail to place their work in publications is that they direct manuscripts to periodicals that go to readers with entirely different interests.

An article about how to cozen chickens to lay more or better eggs may suit a farm magazine but hardly has any place in a women's glossy fashion monthly. When editors tell of the curious stories and articles, totally unfit for their pages, that come in their morning mail, one wonders at the intelligence of some would-be authors.

A matter of simplicity

Once adjustments for the general market were made, I gave more thought to writing style. In English-speaking Western countries there is a school of thought that believes brief, clear, and simple style is important in all writing, be it technical, scholarly, or general.

One holder of that view was Bertrand Russell, the British mathematician, philosopher, and reformer who during his 98 years from 1872 to 1970 became a controversial world figure. But his books and articles could be understood by far more persons than could comprehend most other mathematicians, philosophers, and social reformers.

The talented journalistic writer, I decided, faces the challenge that confronted Russell and some of his equally famous contemporaries, such as George Bernard Shaw and H. G. Wells. (Both were professional essayists as well as social reformers like Russell; Shaw was also a noted dramatist and Wells a novelist.) The journalist must somehow make difficult subjects understandable. Some concepts and ideas, however, cannot be reduced to high school level language, for they require background knowledge that may take years to acquire and understand.

Fortunately for me, my subjects for the most part lent themselves to general treatment: reports on my travels, and observations about the life in my own country as well as in others, particularly the problems plaguing all of us. These are not subjects that require a specialist's expertise to think and write about. I attempted no deep sociological analyses, for I was not competent to do so. I confined myself to readily observable trends, bolstered by the views of genuine experts.

On rejections

One of the deathless witticisms of the writing world is saying that one has had so many rejections that one can paper a room with these slips and sheets. But readers of this book may by now have gained the impression that my writing history has been made up of a lifetime of prompt acceptances of my work and that rejection slips never were in my mail, much less in quantity enough to serve as wall covering.

However, if I had saved all the rejection documents received since I first sold an article as a free-lancer, I am sure that I now could not only paper my study but also other rooms in my house. I have no statistics to support this assertion, but my hundreds of record cards on file, one for every article, book, or other kind of writing I have done, would give me a clue. These cards show how often and far every piece of work traveled before being published, if ever. But I'm too busy writing to do the tabulation.

Although called rejection slips, these cheerless pieces of paper vary in size from 3-by-2-inch all the way to 8½-by-11-inch sheets. Few writers escape receiving them from editors. Many are the tales of writers struggling for a decade to land a piece in print while the "Sorry," "No thanks," and "Not for us" messages pile up year after year.

The two important issues are how to escape rejection and what one can learn from it if faced with it. Avoiding it never can be accomplished 100 percent. But it can be reduced in quantity by consulting editors before writing. Or, if one is competitive enough to have an author's representative, working through that aide's connections. It helps not to rush to put the script in the mail, but to let it lie fallow for a few days and then read it aloud once more.

Also helpful is to pass an idea before an "author's checklist" before the writing actually begins. A few questions to ask are: Is the (book, article, poem, short story, or some other form) fitted to the audience of the periodical or book publishing firm? Is its vocabulary suitable to the readers? Is the central idea original or, if not, treated with an original style?

If the work is still rejected, it should be examined in the light of what, if anything, was said about it. Most editors say nothing or little of help to the writer. It is impossible for them to give personal attention to manuscripts when, as they do in many large editorial offices, unsolicited submissions pour in by the thousands every year, sometimes as many as 50 thousand in the USA.

Until the rejection slips and letters begin to point out the same faults, I consider what comes back as having been *returned*, rather than *rejected*. For there are so many reasons for not publishing any given manuscript. Many pieces are returned because the editorial office already has bought something similar, or one like it was published a year ago, or the editorial budget has just been cut. None of these has anything to do with quality.

Following are a few of the lessons I have learned from my bushels of rejection slips and letters:

Never throw away a returned manuscript unless it is hopelessly outdated. I have placed articles first sent out 15 to 20 years before, with almost no revision.

Have faith in your work. If the writer believes in the script, the fight is worth making.

Admit that the adverse critics may be right. Reread the manuscript as if it were the work of someone else. Take the help of a writers' group in your community, if there is such an organization.

Be grateful to editors who point out weaknesses in manuscripts and encourage writers. I have some old scripts that I am glad never were accepted and published. Years later I saw their faults and thanked the editor for saving me from myself.

In my files are proposals for at least a dozen books I never have written, and scores of full-length articles, written or just proposed, that no editor liked. The writer's occupation indeed would be more pleasant if one were able to publish everything one wrote. After reaching a certain height in the profession, writers are sometimes given that boon. But behind it lies an apprenticeship of years of apparent failure and discouragement symbolized by the hated rejection slip.

Some horror stories

Sometimes rejection comes not from something you have written but from mismanagement. I have been struck with the inefficiency of several book publishing firms in the U.S., India, and Argentina. I have had the same impression while handling the literary affairs of friends or advising strangers who turn to me for help in searching for a publisher. Two instances are typical.

The author of a biography wrote to an editor in the Far East, a European who was much interested in the manuscript, which related to his part of the world. He seemed ready to offer a publishing agreement. Then came a letter announcing his intention to leave the company and start a publishing firm of his own. After months of delay and fruitless efforts to get news through the mail, he informed my friend that he had encountered certain difficulties in starting his venture and could not promise to bring out her manuscript.

He suggested that she turn it over to an author's representative (once called a literary agent) in England. That was done, with more months of delay. After the agent had obtained rejections from three prominent British publishers, she was in an auto accident and not much later bore her first child and decided to give up her agency.

The author, at the agent's suggestion, asked that her manuscript be sent to one of the world famous London representatives, Curtis Brown. After six months, no word had been received from London, even after sending letters of inquiry reinforced with International Reply Coupons to guarantee a reply. Then an unexplained rejection came. Later the author learned that the excuse given was that the manuscript could not be found in the agent's offices. It finally was brought to light with no better verdict.

The second example is even more horrendous in some ways. It is a study by a university scholar of a black pastor and church paper editor of the nineteenth century who lived and worked in both Canada and the USA. Several times this manuscript has been on the verge of acceptance during its tour of publishing houses, religious and secular alike, commercial or nonprofit as well. But only on the verge. These journeys have been going on for four years now, and the author has experienced most of the agonies writers can encounter from inefficient, slovenly editors or other functionaries.

One editor sent a publishing contract and then turned down the book on second thought, before the agreement could be signed. An editor elsewhere held it for a year, despite letters and phone calls; during the conversations he would promise a verdict in two weeks. It took him 12 months of such procrastination to decide no.

Another editor lost it for three months; another time the postal service mangled the script (or the editor's general factotum wrapped it carelessly); one editor wrote a memorandum to the author scolding him for certain small and unimportant alleged grammatical errors and had the gall to scribble all over the script correcting it. It was necessary, then, for the author to retype parts of it. Yet my friend goes on, having spent more on postage than he probably will recover if it ever is published.

These examples are bad enough, but sometimes, ironically, the rejections begin after the book is published. This happened with one book of mine, *The Changing Magazine*.[1] Five years after publication, royalty payments began showing up late or not at all, and I had to send reminders. The next year no payments were made, but I received a letter from the president explaining that because of a shortage of cash flow created by the London operations, there would be a delay.

Indeed there was. That was the last communication I received. I consulted with other of the firm's authors. All had received identical treatment. The firm owed some of them far more than it owed me. We considered hiring a lawyer, but

1. Roland E. Wolseley, *The Changing Magazine* (New York: Hastings House, 1973).

decided the expense probably would wipe out the royalties anyway.[2] Such an experience with a publisher comes under the heading of "the romance of authorship," an ancient expression used by cynical authors who are tired of hearing readers say that writing must be fun with no headaches.

A word for the good editors

To balance this account of the shortcomings of book editors and publishers, I want to relate happy relationships I have had in working with certain editors of my manuscripts. Usually these have been assistant editors. It is the practice in book editorial offices for staff members to be asked to work with certain authors of new books, according to the editor's knowledge of the author's field. Especially is this true if the manuscript is a text or technical book. A number of such editors, at large and small companies, read every word of my manuscripts, some affixing slips of paper to the margins of pages calling attention to errors or challenging assertions.

The best editors I have had, be they chieftains or subordinate chiefs only, are like the best city or metropolitan editors of newspapers or article editors of magazines. Before the author puts fingers to typewriter, they make as clear as they can certain fundamentals. These are what editorial style the author is to follow, the editor's understanding of the scope and nature of the book, hints to where assistance can be obtained from the publisher's office in such matters as help on typing or copying materials and, as with New York publishers, limited amounts of research aid in libraries and other sources difficult for the author to visit personally.

Such an editor also sees to it that there is clear understanding of the expected length of the script, who is to prepare the index and by what method, and as nearly as can be estimated, what the flow of proofs will be so that the author need not cancel his trip to Ecuador (to research another book) while awaiting the page proofs on the present one.

A few larger companies put much of this guidance into a booklet published solely for their authors. Others are content to direct their authors to the style manual of the University of

---

2. In summer 1983 Hastings House filed in bankruptcy court in New York, and its authors were given the opportunity to file claims. Total royalty indebtedness to authors amounted to a half million dollars; installments of percentage payments began in 1984.

Chicago Press or the McGraw-Hill company's similar volume. Such road signs can keep an author from going along the wrong highway and save editors from the tedious work of changing scores of inconsistencies in style. (Is it Clark Avenue or Clark avenue? 102nd St. or One-hundred second street? The Reverend John Axminster or just Rev.?)

I am grateful to other editors because they answered letters promptly, even telephoned instead of using the mail to help me. Others have provided hard-to-spot photographs or expedited permission-to-quote letters.

And here is my opportunity to praise the religion publishing business in the USA, including both book and magazine firms. I have had some problems with editors being eternally slow with decisions, reports, and payment, but only a few have so transgressed. And none who ignored their agreements. Almost all have been businesslike, helpful, and pleasant.

Some staff members on the business side of publishing also have earned my admiration. Publishers commonly ask authors to supply lists of friends or other persons to whom direct mail advertising may be sent. Or names of publications that might print reviews. I have made several dozen such lists but few company publicity and public relations or advertising and promotion offices have made more than casual use of them. Three times, however, I have received my original list back, with check marks to show which persons or places were followed up. Two of these were small houses; one was among the biggest in the USA.

All such good work takes intelligent organization of the intricate book-making process, especially the work with the author. It takes a genuine interest in the book itself, a desire to make it a successful one for the author, the company, and the particular editor or publicity director.

12   On Free-lancing and Books

*Knowing your strengths and weaknesses
as a writer. Creativity in journalism.
Lessons learned as a free-lancer.
Helpful books on writing and teaching.*

I anticipated that in retirement my writing environment would change drastically. I looked forward to the chance to write what I wanted to write and read what I wanted to read. Not that I did not enjoy my writing and reading up to that time. Since 1937, free-lance writing always had been done as an adjunct of my main job—teaching. Therefore I wrote at night, on weekends, and during vacations. The only concentrated time I had most of my 35 years as a full-time teacher was during the few leaves of absence I obtained. But after 1969 I would follow a different pattern, writing taking at least half my time. I had to adjust, also, to the need to take more responsibility at home. My wife had serious health problems, and I was needed more than before.

Not only was my daily routine changing but so also were my associations. I would spend much less time with colleagues and students, thereby losing the companionship and stimulation of being with people.

I now was presented with a dilemma. For most of my professional life I had concentrated heavily on different aspects of journalism. Was I willing to let up on those specialties and be content with writing travel articles and occasional pieces on public issues of particular importance to me? Was I willing to do the background study travel writing requires? Would I willingly absent myself from my offices and home and professional routines to do more visiting of other lands as well as see parts of my own new to me?

As it turned out, I have managed to continue giving considerable attention to developments in old specialties. It is not as much as before, but enough to let me think I am keeping up-to-date. I continue to read as many of the new books touching my journalistic interests as I can find. I subscribe still to the more important journals and other periodicals of print journalism. And I still clip and file.

My travel and nonjournalism resources both have been enlarged. Already having spread my office to the library I now found myself using the dining room as an adjunct also. After awhile I began thinking of broadening my field of interest still more.

Other questions arise

I pondered, also, a challenge. Might this time in my life be perhaps my opportunity to write not only about religion and communications but also about religion itself? Certainly as a churchman I had long held views that I desired to express about problems within the religious world—the meaning of the sacrifice of Jesus to the daily lives of people today, the duty of Christians in a pagan world, how valid it is to expect religions, Christianity or any other, to include the ideal of nonviolent resistance to war and to other social evils.

But as I dwelt on these ideas I realized that I had nothing new to say. I had no original ideas, no cures for mankind's ills that had not been explored endlessly for years. I did not give up completely, but could not see a program of religion writing on substantive topics more than occasionally, as some experience, perhaps, stimulated me. I realized that I was not well grounded enough in theology or church history to set myself up as a writer on strictly religious topics. As it turned out, however, I would do more such writing than I had expected and also far more with manuscripts on religious communications.

I also faced another challenge, this one far different. I had faced it before. Should I attempt fiction? All my life I had read novels and short stories and had written a number of stories but published only a few. It was an appealing idea. I made stabs at new tales but bumped into the old obstacles once more.

They arose from the fact that a writer brought up on journalism, either as an occupation or a subject for teaching (in my case both) finds it difficult to write fiction. Many story writers have overcome that handicap but I have not—yet.

The journalist is taught to cleave to the truth, to reality, to shun imagining events, and to invent nothing. As we know from occasional violations by writers on the staffs of some of our greatest daily papers, some journalists do break the rules. The fiction writer may be inspired by real life persons and situations, but he or she cannot be content to be a reporter. Certain events must be shuffled to heighten the drama of conflict. Characters must communicate, so dialogue must be invented. New characters sometimes must be added to the cast to bring out particular points or to serve as foils for others. All these must be born in the writer's brain.

Such devices were unnatural to me and went against the grain. Especially difficult was remembering the elementary techniques: to write using all the senses and not just sight, for instance. Or constructing dialogue so that it sounded natural without being a literal copy of what had been picked up by a tape recorder. Thus I made the decision to leave fiction to the days when I no longer could get about and my imagination might compensate for being housebound.

In defense of creative journalism

Yet I found myself defending journalism as essentially creative when it was attacked as uncreative. And I still am its champion when so charged. A typical instance of this occurred one day after church. During the coffee hour a fellow member introduced a young woman attending the service, a visitor. After the exchange of names I asked if she was a student. She was, and at Syracuse.

"What department or school?"

"Arts and Science."

"Good," I said. "Major?"

"English."

"Well. That brings you close to my school, Newhouse."

"Oh, no," she said. "I'm interested in creative writing."

Creative got all the stress.

That was a familiar comment, so I went right on.

"You think that journalism isn't creative, then?"

"It's not writing poetry or short stories or novels."

"That's true. But why do you think there's no creativity in journalism?"

"It's all facts. No imagination. Nothing is created. It's just reporting."

"Did you ever write a magazine article?" I asked.

"No."

"Do you know how one is written?"

"No, I guess I really don't."

So I related the genesis of an article of mine, although I did not tell her it was written by me. The writer had an idea. In his mind's eye he could see the main point or theme, I explained. I went on to tell how the writer began research on the idea. He read certain books and articles, took notes on four-by-six-inch cards, interviewed a half-dozen experts on the subject, several of them by mail. He assembled all this information. Then I stopped, leaving out the rest of the procedure.

"Now, wasn't that being creative?" I asked. In other words, that writer took a mere idea and produced something concrete from it, just as a short story writer gets a glimpse of insight into life and builds a tale around it.

She agreed. And as a form of making amends for her slighting the creative possibilities of journalism, she added another remark.

"My fiance is in Newhouse and he says the same thing."

And then she walked off, satisfied with her creative self.

Scores of advisees at the several universities where I have taught have made similar comments to me about creativity. They forget the many noted authors who were journalists first and were trained as writers on newspapers and magazines: Ernest Hemingway, Edgar Allan Poe, Henry L. Mencken, Theodore Dreiser, William Cullen Bryant, Bret Hart, and Truman Capote are among them.

Risks and rewards of the free-lancer

My article writing was intensified somewhat in the late 1970s when I came to know Jack Wood, editor and publisher at the time of *Freelancer's Newsletter*. This newsletter carried articles of interest mainly to independent writers, photographers, and editors as well as reports on needs of publications, particularly new ones. It then was published 22 times a year but since has become a monthly.

After I had contributed a few pieces, Wood invited more short articles about various aspects of free-lance writing. (See appendix 1.) My copy was in most of the issues from 1978 to early 1982. Through this, I had an outlet for accounts of my own ongoing free-lancing as well as of my earlier writing experiences of possible interest to FN's readers. Occasionally I included results of surveys I made in the area of manuscript marketing and reports on newspaper and magazine dealings with free-lance writers.

After more than 50 years of free-lance writing in several journalistic and literary forms, one should be a past master of it or at least have had many professional experiences, some of which may be useful to other writers. I am no master, past or present, but as a writer I have had some experiences dealing with editors. Knowing about these may help other unattached writers by cheering them on or warning them of pitfalls.

All free-lancers for magazines can tell stories of editorial abuses, dishonesty, or what seems like downright stupidity. (See previous chapter.) Similarly, all can tell stories of fair and considerate treatment, since that is the norm. The negative happenings make better stories, however, being more dramatic.

I sent an article to a writer's magazine and heard nothing of it for months. Letters of inquiry were ignored. About the time I had given up, I was looking at the offerings of a newsstand and saw a new magazine for authors issued by the same firm. On its cover was a listing of my article. I was never able to collect payment. But that was not the end of the matter.

A year or so later I saw a new magazine devoted to opinion articles to which I had sent a contribution and again had heard nothing, having seen an announcement of its publication in advance. Six issues later, once more passing that newsstand, there was the new issue with a listing of my article on its cover. And once again, although this was a different company, I was unable to collect payment or receive any explanation.

But I did get some return by writing of these two experiences for the *Writer* magazine and was paid for that piece. Why did I not sue the first two companies? Because it costs too much to hire an attorney to bring pressure to bear on careless or dishonest publishing firms. Sometimes their owners know that and take advantage of it.

On the other hand, I sent a certain article, unchanged, each year for three years in succession, to a specialized magazine of business. It was rejected twice and accepted on the third try. Moral: never give up. Conditions can change, the public's interest or taste alters. Or the publication no longer is overstocked.

For a time I published the same article simultaneously in as many as 15 different magazines of religion. That is possible because members of one denomination rarely read the magazines of another. It is like self-syndication and involves the sale of second rights. It widens the readership of one's work and also multiplies the payment for it. One time an editor wrote me a letter saying he would like to buy second rights to a piece of mine he had seen in some other denomination's publication. What he overlooked was that he had bought it from me already and even paid for it, but forgotten he had it in his inventory. Or maybe some assistant editor had bought it and failed to list it.

I have had a few editors pay me twice for the same piece of work, many not at all, and some call or write me after rejecting a piece because they had changed their minds. One was in such a hurry that she telephoned from Florida to New York to request that I send the article by special delivery. A travel magazine editor, using my return envelope, sent me in it a piece by another author whose work was being rejected. Under the same paper clip was an article of mine. I called attention to this conjunction, and was told to send on the rejected piece. With a new stamped envelope the editor enclosed, I mailed back my article, which later was published.

Almost anything can happen in a world where both writers and editors are handling so much material. Mix-ups and mistakes occur easily. When things work out favorably, it offsets the disappointments that come from rejection.

A writer's library

On turning into virtually a full-time free-lance writer during retirement, I naturally reviewed my library holdings on literary techniques—a collection of books filling two 3½-foot wide shelves. Three additional 2½-foot wide shelves contain books on specialized writing—news writing, magazine article writing, journalistic criticism, and other special types. Another half of one of the wider shelves has books on teaching and education.

In all of these shelves, I keep volumes that were important and helpful to me years ago as well as more recent ones that are currently useful. I list most of these below; others are in footnotes in earlier chapters. Many no longer are in print, although now and then one of the older ones is republished or updated. Many can be found in any well-stocked university, college, or large city library, particularly in institutions that offer courses in communications.

Writing

Barzun, Jacques. *Simple and Direct*. New York: Harper and Row, 1969.

Bernstein, Theodore M. *The Careful Writer*. New York: Atheneum, 1965.

————. *Watch Your Language*. Great Neck, N.Y.: Channel Press, 1958.

————. *More Language That Needs Watching*. Great Neck, N.Y.: Channel Press, 1962.

Bowen, Catherine Drinker. *The Writing of Biography*. Boston: The Writer, Inc., 1952.

————. *Biography: The Craft and the Calling*. Boston: Little, Brown & Co., 1969.

Bremner, John B. *Words on Words*. New York: Columbia University Press, 1980.

Brittain, Vera. *On Being an Author*. New York: Macmillan, 1948.

Ferguson, Charles W. *Say It with Words*. New York: Alfred A. Knopf, Inc., 1959.

Fowler, H. W. *A Dictionary of Modern English Usage*. 2nd ed. New York: Oxford University Press, 1965. See Nicholson below.

Frankau, Pamela. *Pen to Paper: A Novelist's Notebook*. New York: Doubleday & Co., Inc., 1962.

Gentz, William, ed. *Writing to Inspire*. Cincinnati, Ohio: Writer's Digest Books, 1982.

Nicholson, Margaret. *A Dictionary of American-English Usage*. New York: Oxford University Press, 1957.

Based on Fowler's *Modern English Usage* listed above.

O'Hara, Mary. *Novel-in-the-Making*. New York: David McKay Co., Inc., 1954.

Rivers, William L. *Writing: Craft and Art*. Englewood Cliffs, N.J.: Prentice-Hall, Inc., 1975.

Rosenbaum, Jean, and Veryl Rosenbaum. *The Writer's Survival Guide*. Cincinnati, Ohio: Writer's Digest Books, 1982.

Weeks, Edward. *Breaking into Print: An Editor's Advice on Writing*. Boston: The Writer, Inc., 1962.

Scores of biographies of writers of many kinds of material are helpful because they often describe their working methods. They are too numerous to be listed in full here. Among those useful to me have been the biographies and autobiographies of:

Lyman Abbott	Briton Hadden
Ray Stannard Baker	Ernest Hemingway
Ambrose Bierce	H. L. Mencken
Bruce Bliven	Phyllis Reynolds Naylor
Stephen Crane	Edgar Allan Poe
Dorothy Day	Burton Rascoe
Theodore Dreiser	Kenneth Roberts
Edna Ferber	Harold Ross
Gene Fowler	Mark Twain
Benjamin Franklin	John A. Williams
Paul Gallico	

Only a few books on teaching at the university level are available. I wanted to contribute to that sparse literature by writing a Ph.D. dissertation on the practical aspects of teaching journalism, but was refused approval for the very reason that it was too practical. The few books that I found helpful were biographical or autobiographical and largely offering inspiration. Only one was useful to me in solving everyday problems, that of Luella Cole. Following are those in my library.

Teaching

Barzun, Jacques. *Teacher in America*. Boston: Atlantic Monthly, Little, Brown & Co., 1945.

Cole, Luella. *The Background for College Teaching*. New York: Farrar & Rinehart, 1941.

Edman, Irwin. *Philosopher's Holiday*. New York: Penguin Books, 1938.

Peterson, Houston, ed. *Great Teachers*. New Brunswick, N.J.: Rutgers University Press, 1946.

Much about both teaching and writing can be learned from books. Teaching still is poorly supplied. Writing, on the other hand, has a rich bibliography, covering all aspects of literary craftsmanship and journalistic techniques.

But such books can go only so far in helping would-be authors or teachers. Experienced craftsmen and women can pass along useful, tested working methods on innumerable aspects of both occupations. They can, but in teaching rarely do.

Greatness in either teacher or writer cannot be imparted by books, for that is by individual endowment. But, as with singers and other musicians, books can save the artist from making serious mistakes early in a career. Or, books can teach the craft of writing but not the art of writing. The practicing journalist or author moving into the classroom needs books of this type but also some that discuss educational philosophy or theory.

13   Inspiration and Solitude

Writers who have been friends—
Elizabeth Yates, Frank Luther Mott,
R. K. Narayan, Charles W. Ferguson.
The single life again.

Writers themselves and not only their books and biographies have been inspirational. I have made little effort to come to know them by joining writers' organizations or going to meetings. Instead I have had as friends a few talented writers who by example held me to my purposes.

One of these is Elizabeth Yates—novelist, biographer, children's book writer, and author of various nonfiction volumes not so easily classified. She has published more than half a hundred books to this writing. We became acquainted in the 1950s through the Green Lake Christian Writers' Conference and to this day correspond about each other's writing activities.

What impresses me most strongly about Elizabeth Yates's work is its consistent high-mindedness. Everything she writes has a helpful purpose. But first of all it is good writing. She avoids drippy sentimentalism, so often the bane of writers who have a sense of mission about their work. She is a positive, constructive person.

Her book *Call It Zest* is an example. It encourages older persons to use their talents as long as they can. Another is *The*

Lighted Heart, perhaps the one of her many books that will live longest. In it she describes how she and William McGreal, her husband, met the reality of his blindness and their adjustment to it and the building of a new life in the face of the sudden change in his existence. *Up the Golden Stair*, written after his death, is an encouraging book for persons who must deal with the loss of a loved one. It reports her own thoughts as well as the ideas of little-known and famous writers on death.

Elizabeth Yates's books are helpful on personal problems and also are concerned with society's problems in general. Her pioneering book for young people, *Amos Fortune, Free Man*, first published in 1950, was issued when it was not yet common to champion black people in their fight for equality in the American democracy. It won her a Newbery Award the year after publication and has gone into many printings since, becoming a classic in literature for what are called older children. Others of her books with social import are *Prudence Crandall, Woman of Courage* and *Howard Thurman, Portrait of a Practical Dreamer*. Elizabeth Yates's understanding attitude toward people in minority groups helped me to find my own way in the race relations controversy.

No matter what she undertakes to write, Elizabeth Yates is painstaking and thorough about details. A good deal of her nonfiction for both adults and young persons proves that. *With Pipe, Paddle and Song*, an account of the French-Canadian voyageurs of the middle nineteenth century, is typical. How she had the idea for this book is a story in itself.

She was on vacation in northern Minnesota at Gunflint and Grand Marais. On a canoe trip with a friend and a guide, she learned about the voyageurs, who were canoeists in the North American fur trade and famed for their singing.

While staying at the hotel in Grand Marais, she was given in fun the figure of a voyageur about eight inches high, in a red hat, blue jacket, and a plaid sash around his waist. His leggings, mittens, and shoes were tan. In his hands was a typical short paddle used by canoeists then. His black hair was down to his shoulders.

When the figure was handed to her, her companion on the trip, Dr. Mary Griffin, also an author, asked Elizabeth what she would call the little voyageur. She answered instantly, "Guillaume Puissante." He became her central character. She proceeded to do elaborate research to give veracity to such factors as setting, geography, dress, food, and weather, for example.

An outdoors person all her life and a lover of nature and animals, Elizabeth Yates wrote for years in a hidden room at the back of a landmark house. She and her husband lived on the outskirts of Peterborough, New Hampshire, a typical New England town with a tall, white steepled church. After her husband's death she moved her workroom to the upstairs front and had more room, and better light.

In *Call It Zest* she explains in a colophon[1] that during 17 interviews with persons over 70, she took few notes for the book. She did not, she explained, wish to impede the natural, easy flow of conversation. On returning home she wrote down everything that was said, as faithfully as her memory would permit. These first drafts were sent to the protagonists. They were returned with corrections. What pleased her most was that seeing the drafts stimulated many of these persons to add more material.

A scholar's library

Another personal influence upon me was Frank Luther Mott, the widely recognized historian of American newspapers and magazines and a distinguished teacher and administrator in several of the larger schools of journalism in the USA.

I first met this jovial man at an annual meeting of the Association for Education in Journalism[2] and saw him frequently thereafter at other AEJ sessions as well as at other professional gatherings. I came to know him more personally in Columbia, Missouri, site of the University of Missouri, because I was at the university as a member of an accreditation team. But I really was far more interested in seeing Frank Mott than in anything else I was doing on the visit.

He had invited me to call on him at his home the evening of my arrival. When I walked into the hallway, I glanced at the television set in the living room and saw on the screen a scene of Syracuse in the middle of a great blizzard. It had started after I had left the East. I soon submerged this worry when, after a

1. An explanation at the end of a book of how it was written or produced.
2. Recently this was expanded to the Association for Education in Journalism and Mass Communication.

time, Frank took me downstairs to his library and office. It was lined floor to ceiling with book shelving. At one side were his desk and typewriter and a low file cabinet. The portable must have been of 1920 or 1930 vintage—a spindly little machine it was. He said he had done much of his writing on it, including parts of what became a six-volume history of U.S. magazines that brought him a Pulitzer prize for history.

I modeled the small lower floor library in my Syracuse house after the Mott room, although my desks, working file cabinets, and typewriters are in a study on the floor above. As his book collection must have done for him, mine has saved me innumerable hours of searching in libraries. A large number of my professional books are not in any of the Syracuse libraries; my collection on the press of India is matched in only a few places in the USA.

In addition to his library, I admired Frank Mott's tireless research and his respect for scholarly accuracy. Sometimes, when tempted not to check a date or some other statement of fact, I remember his meticulous work.

A taste of his diligence is provided in *Time Enough: Essays in Autobiography*, where he writes about a principle he followed: "Anyone has time enough for anything he really wants to do. Anything within reason, of course, and under ordinary circumstances. One must make one's choices. Anything a person wants to do, if he wants hard enough to do it and if it is within his powers, he will find time for."[3]

Narayan and Ferguson

R. K. Narayan of India is another writer who has deeply impressed me. He is his country's outstanding English-language novelist. He has made the imagined village of Malgudi more real to me through his short novels about it and its people than many of the small towns I visit now and then near Syracuse.

Narayan's books are being republished from time to time in the USA and the U.K. and hardly a year goes by that he has not been honored by another literary award. Fair samples of his work are *The Man-Eater of Malgudi*, *Mr. Sampath*, *The Vendor of Sweets*, *Swami and Friends*, and *The Financial Expert*. I link his work with that of the American novelist, Sherwood Ander-

---

3. Frank Luther Mott, *Time Enough: Essays in Autobiography* (Chapel Hill, N.C.: University of North Carolina Press, 1962), 239.

son, but only in the apt use of locale. Another comparison, more appropriate perhaps, can be made with V. S. Naipaul, whose stories of Trinidad are not as humorous and gentle as Narayan's but just as full of insight into obscure people and their lives.

Narayan helps me to remember always that the people who live in the streets near me comprise my immediate world. They are my real companions. In his short autobiographical book[4], he describes how he fell in love with the daughter of a neighbor after ogling other girls all over the town. She had been there all the time. After much family opposition, they finally were married.

We met while I was visiting various publishing establishments in India; during my stop in Mysore I sought him out. He was friendly and certainly unaware that he would become a world literary figure several decades later. (See appendix 1 for an article about him I subsequently contributed to the *Nation*.)

Most of what little fiction I have attempted to write is frankly imitative of the Narayan-Naipaul-Anderson school. Perhaps that is why a little of it has been published in India.

Perhaps of more direct influence was my acquaintance with Charles W. Ferguson, long a senior editor of *Reader's Digest* and a clergyman before he entered the book and magazine publishing worlds. He was a favorite speaker at religion writers' conferences.

He was a forerunner of the modern word-book writers: William Safire, Edwin Newman, and John Simon are among the better known. Note the titles of some of Ferguson's books: *Say It with Words*, *The Abcedarian Book*, and *A Is for Advent*. But he will be remembered longer, perhaps, for his masterwork, *Naked to Mine Enemies: The Life of Cardinal Wolsey*. We talked often about his work on this book, on which he spent years working in England. The research and travel he did in connection with it were prodigious. When his son Hugh came to Syracuse University to study I came to know Charlie still better.

Unlike some other authors I have known personally, Charlie was a good listener. He volunteered little about himself and his work but asked many questions about the activities of the person he was talking with. And when you answered, he nodded

4. R. K. Narayan, *My Days: A Memoir* (New York: Viking Press, 1973).

in appreciation but not necessarily in agreement with your observations and opinions. I remember one train trip we made together during which he sat facing me, and when I talked in answer to his questions, he nodded and took occasional notes for most of the six-hour journey.

He awakened further my sensitivity to words. Take as an example his explanation of the main word in the title of his book *The Abecedarian Book*. He points out that "Big words make nice noises," and goes on to note that there are more sounds in the word *hippopotamus* than in *cat*, more in *allegory* than in *tale*. He urges learning big words because in doing so one comes to know more since most large words are related to other words. He then notes that abecedarian is an actual word, more than 300 years old, and refers to someone who is learning or teaching the ABC's.

The English language was his favorite subject in his speeches for writers' conferences. Some speakers on language can lose their listeners by going into too much detail and using too many examples, but never Charlie Ferguson. He mixed humor with his tracing of word derivation.

Death in the family

All this inspiration, whatever its source, was not enough to offset the shattering shock of the death of my wife, Bernice, after knowing her for 55 years and being married to her for nearly 52 of them. She died in October 1980.

Even if I could describe the effect of this upon me I would not want to relate it. Such an event brings one face to face with reality as almost nothing else can. And when one is alone, as I was after she was taken by leukemia, only one's faith, family, and friends can be of help, and the burden fell upon the first and the last, since family we had virtually none. Happy memories also help one through the nightmare and of these I had many.

For the first time since my school and college days I was forced to live alone. Being in a house with no one else is not the same as having a room in someone else's house. In the latter case, other people are around much of the time and close friendships can be formed. In fact, it was that way that I first came to know my wife.

All responsibilities were now upon me: maintaining the house, keeping the accounts, housecleaning, cooking, bill paying, repairs, and other chores. Some of these duties I had never had to contend with. One of the most arduous was figuring the income taxes and filling in the forms. My brainy wife had all our lives together taken care of such financial records and duties. This work, in addition to writing, giving lectures, teaching, and travel, kept me busy.

I wish I could end this last chapter on a clearly upbeat note. I have attempted a passage of that nature. Repeatedly it sounded to me like platitudes. This reluctance to say the bromidic comes from all my experiences in life and from my belief in a religion of depth. Such a religion finds that the answers to life's problems are not always easy, and this compels me to look to the past and to the future realistically.

If I did not have hope I could not persist, so it is obvious that I have it. It rests upon belief in the existence of God as spirit in a troubled world, on the power of the Christian church for good when it chooses to exercise it, and on the persistent good deeds of people in a world that still makes the doing of evil far too easy.

Epilogue

Despite what is said at the end of chapter 13, certain events have made it possible for me to conclude on a clearly upbeat note.

Several such notes, in fact.

I married again and so an end has come to my loneliness.

A publisher offered to bring out a book I long have wanted to prepare.

Because the ministry and members of Erwin United Methodist Church in Syracuse have been so helpful to me, especially in recent years, I became a member in full standing.

My other activities have continued despite my retirement. I continue to write books, articles, and reviews, to engage in church work, and to travel, such as a trip in 1984 to China. Such activities differ mainly in detail and degree—and in the fact that I share them with someone else.

My second wife, Isabel Champ Wolseley, is also a writer. Since 1971, she has been writing articles for leading religious periodicals and contributing to religious books. For a decade, she turned out three different columns a week for dailies and weeklies in Oregon. Before this, she worked in radio and television. It is clear that we have many interests in common. We met, in fact, at a religion writers' conference, where we both were on the faculty.

These days we work together in a house cluttered more than ever with books and magazines and equipped with a second electric typewriter. Our first joint product as authors is a book appearing about the same time as this one. It is the eighth edition of *The Journalist's Bookshelf*. A reference work of nearly 400 pages, it is subtitled *An Annotated and Critical Bibliography of United States Print Journalism*.

There is much work left to do before I go out of print.

Afterword

Editor's note. While Roland Wolseley was completing the manuscript for Still in Print, *we asked a number of his former students to comment on the impact he has had on them as teacher, fellow writer, leader in religion journalism, and friend. Following are their responses.*

Lutrelle F. Palmer, Jr., and I came north to Syracuse from Virginia during the exciting postwar years of 1946-48. We were the School of Journalism's first black candidates for master's degrees. Professor Wolseley, a new member of the respected journalism faculty, proved to be the complete teacher: goal-conscious, thorough, provocative, exacting, and innovative. His outlook was cosmopolitan, and he opened new vistas of international communication.

O. RUDOLPH AGGREY
Former U.S. Ambassador to Senegal
The Gambia, and Romania

Roland Wolseley's standards of excellence, his emphasis on treating schoolwork "professionally," and his dedication to hard work made lasting impressions. But it is in the long and close correspondence we have maintained since school days that Roland Wolseley has done what so few teachers are willing or able to do: he has shared his life and experience with great depth and honesty, forsaking the pedestal of professorship for the common ground of friendship.

MARGARET E. BAILEY
Managing Editor
World Press Review

My first week in Professor Wolseley's magazine class, I submitted a paper in which I said I'd "poured over" certain reading material (instead of "pored"). The returned paper had in its margin, "Was it coffee you poured?" That was only the beginning. By the time I left Dr. Wolseley's classes some four years later, my writing (and spelling) skills had been sharpened, and I was well on my way toward the career in dictionary work of which I'd dreamed.

RUTH KIMBALL KENT
Associate Editor
Webster's New World Dictionary

Dr. Wolseley has been my concerned, helpful mentor in religion journalism since 1949. His continual correspondence evaluating practically all of my thousands of newspaper and magazine articles and book reviews has helped me learn to accept criticism and grow. He always has been rigorous. After one forthright, negative evaluation of one of my weaker articles, he followed his letter with a postcard a week later with the brief question, "Have you bounced back yet?"

JAMES. W. CARTY, JR.
Professor of Communications
Bethany College, Bethany, West Virginia

Roland E. Wolseley's standards as a teacher were high. Although I never dreamed I'd teach, I never forgot his example. I took every course he taught, and I lived for his comments on my reporting and interpretative articles. Today, when I manage to teach or write in a way that I respect, I always wish I could share my good fortune with him.

RICHARD H. COSTA
Author, Professor of English
Texas A & M University

As a pioneer in religion journalism, Dr. Wolseley has produced many pioneers in the Third World who have in turn been able to serve thousands of people in many countries. When I went to Syracuse in 1954 it was the first time abroad for me, full of surprises, pleasant and unpleasant, besides acute homesickness. Dr. Wolseley was one teacher who took as much interest in my personal needs and problems as in my studies. One gloomy winter evening, when I could no longer bear to sit alone by the window and watch the snow fall, I telephoned Dr. Wolseley that I was coming to his house to which he promptly said, "Welcome." He and Mrs. Wolseley received me graciously, and Mrs. Wolseley prepared coffee the South Indian way to make my joy complete. As I walked back to my room, it was still snowing, but now I watched it with fascination as it fell like granulated sugar in the light of the street lamp.

> J. VICTOR KOILPILLAI
> Christian Institute for the Study of Religion
> and Society, Bangalore, India

At the classroom podium, my first day of Roland Wolseley's creative writing course at Northwestern, stood a short man with tousled hair, one foot cocked upward behind the other, eyes so deep and tired that we thought he must have been reading student papers all night every night. It didn't take us long to realize we were in the hands of a remarkable teacher. He never taught me how to write; instead he pushed me to assess my own abilities--and limitations--and to do my very best within that self-scrutiny.

> CLIFFORD B. HICKS
> Author, former editor, *Popular Mechanics*
> Editor, *Popular Mechanics Encyclopedia*

Casual, quiet, and yet firm, very firm, about how you work at the job of writing, how you get at the facts, and how you put those facts together for a readable article—that was Roland Wolseley's style. He gave to us, by example, the formula to work, work, write, write. His greatest way of assisting us as students was the process of critical analysis of the writing that we presented in his class. Sometimes this was a bit rough on unpolished young people, but that part of his sharing remains so much a part of me to this day. And that is the part that still challenges me when I read manuscripts, or when I am in consultation with an editor of a church periodical in India, in Zimbabwe, or in Liberia.

DORIS E. HESS
Communications Executive, World Division
United Methodist Board of Global Ministries

As a new graduate student, I joined a group of brown baggers who gathered daily for lunch and conversation with Professor Wolseley. It was there that I began to develop an appreciation for his character. As a scholar, he is thoughtful, thorough, hardworking and intellectually curious—all admirable qualities but not always found in combination with the character traits that make a completely admirable individual. As a person, Professor Wolseley displays a genuine feeling for moral issues while setting an example of honesty and integrity.

SHERILYN COX BENNION
Professor of Journalism
Humboldt State University, Arcata, California

I chose Professor Roland E. Wolseley for my faculty advisor on arrival at Syracuse University in 1966. A fortuitous choice. Not only did he publish widely and well, he took a personal interest in students, graduate and undergraduate, that drew my professional admiration and deep respect. Authoritative in his field, interesting in his lectures, he expected the best from his students. Through his encouraging letters during many years, I have come to consider him a friend.

REV. JAMES P. COLLIGAN
Asia correspondent for Catholic News Services
Tokyo, Japan

While a graduate student at Syracuse, I was asked to teach journalism at the newly created Africa Literature Centre in Kitwe, Zambia. I discussed the assignment with Professor Wolseley. "Bengt," I remember him saying, "if you are asked to do administrative work, always remember never, never to let go of teaching completely. The teaching is the important work.'' I soon discovered the wisdom of these words. *Get as close to the heart of the matter as you can* was the principle behind them. How often have I not myself said that to students in Africa and in Sweden and to my colleagues here in Stockholm. How often have I not repeated it for myself. For the very kernel in the teaching of Professor Wolseley was just that: Accuracy, use firsthand sources, go to the center of the event. And in your own life, have whatever attitude you will, but let it be yours, not a secondhand one and in your Christian faith show both your belief and your doubts.

BENGT SIMONSSON
Editor, *Energy Teknik, Energy Technology*
News from the Church of Sweden
Stockholm, Sweden

Appendix 1

Roland E. Wolseley in Print

Narayan of India
Reprinted with permission from *The Nation*, October 3, 1953.

R. K. Narayan, one of India's English-language novelists and short-story writers of consequence, who has just been introduced to American readers, has won admiration and respect in Europe but comparatively little attention in his own country.

Just before going to Mysore City in southern India to see Narayan, I stopped at one of the largest English-language bookstores in Bangalore, a city of 750,000, about sixty miles from Mysore in the same province. I asked for some of Narayan's novels, in preparation for an interview with him. His new book "The Financial Expert," recently issued in the United States, had just been published in England and put on sale in India, but there was not a Narayan book in the shop, one of a chain.

"All sold out?"

"No," the manager said, "we have so few calls we do not stock his books."

"But Mr. Narayan is one of India's own novelists. He lives nearby in Mysore City. You display all these new British and American novels, why not his new one?"

The manager was indifferent. "Yes, I know, but we do not read much fiction here in India," he said.

From what the bookstores, railway stalls, and curbstone displays show the public, it is evident that he is right only in part, for the Indians buy American and British novels and short stories as readily as any other people. But it is true that India's own writers are neglected. Mulk Raj Anand, Babani Bhattacharya, whose "Music for Mohini" appeared in the United States last year, and Narayan are the leading Indian writers in English but they must depend upon Europe for recognition equal to their talent.

I asked Narayan for his explanation of this situation. "Frankly," he replied, "there is no publishing business worth mentioning in India. A few enterprising publishers started with hope but have received little material support, public or private. Writing has to be a part-time job in most cases; so a publisher cannot expect steady industry on the part of his writers." He could have added that not more than 15 percent of the people of India are literate and that only 2 percent of these are capable of using English.

Narayan is resigned to his relative obscurity in his own country, in part because he has been received so warmly in England, where all his novels and collections of short stories have been published and widely praised. Graham Greene has been one of the most enthusiastic admirers of his work. "I owe my literary career to Graham Greene's interest in my work," he told me. "He has encouraged me for nearly twenty years now, although we have never met. I consider Graham not only the finest writer but also the finest and most perfect friend a man can have in this world."

Narayan inspires friendship. I met him at the new house overlooking Mysore City that he rented to Dr. Henry Hart, a visiting Fulbright professor from the University of Wisconsin serving on the faculty of the University of Mysore during 1952-53. He came to Professor and Mrs. Hart's home in a gray jacket, a short version of the dignified Indian *sherwani* worn by men of position, gray trousers, and black shoes. His gentleness impressed the Americans who had assembled to meet him but was belied by his lively brown eyes. He is a slight, trim man of forty-five with aquiline features, gracious, modest, and professional in manner. He drew on his experience as a teacher in his somewhat tragic novel, *The English Teacher*, his favorite because it is more personal than the others.

Born in Madras, Narayan attended a Mysore high school of which his father was headmaster, and then went to the University of Mysore. His wife is dead, and he is devoted to his sixteen-year-old daughter, Hema; they live with his mother and brothers in the joint family arrangement so common in India still.

His first book, *Swami and Friends*, was published in 1935 in England by Hamish Hamilton. Like most of the five novels and three collections of short stories that followed, it is about the lives of typical South Indian people: there is not a snake charmer prominent in the lot. Eyre and Spottiswoode of London published *The Bachelor of Arts* two years later; it was reprinted in 1949 and became a British Pocket Book in 1951; next year it is to be published in the United States. *The Dark Room* followed from Macmillan in 1938; *The English Teacher* appeared in 1945, *Mr. Sampath* in 1949, *The Financial Expert* last year, and in between came three collections of short stories. Most of the tales, which have wide variety of subject and method, appeared first in the *Hindu*, India's outstanding English-language daily. A few of these books were published in India also by a small Mysore firm. Reviews there have been enthusiastic but not uncritical. A new novel, now in progress, is about a dissolute character who is influenced by the life of Gandhi, a subject which possibly will bring him for the first time into close touch with India's national problems. Narayan is known for his interest in personal rather than social problems.

What can American readers expect when Narayan's books appear? The novels will be issued regularly now, since the Michigan State University Press, which on October 15 is bringing out *The English Teacher* under the title *Grateful to Life and Death*, plans to publish one old and one new Narayan work each year. Readers will find the writing artistic, quiet in tone and with a flowing rhythm. The plots are slender, based on middle-class Indian life in a mythical community near Madras. Both setting and characters, Narayan said, started from real places and persons but developed characteristics of their own. His subjects are the difficulties and pleasures of life under Indian marriage customs, business methods, and the educational system. *Mr. Sampath* is almost a pure satire on Indian journalism and the film industry.

"The most recurring theme," Narayan said in answer to a question about the favorite themes of India's novelists, "has been the suffering of the individual under social and political injustices. Some have chosen romantic-historical subjects, and a few have reminisced charmingly about their community or village."

Which themes have been neglected? "I fear that the rich subjective life of an individual against the background of that unique institution, the joint family system, is a subject that has not been properly tackled," he replied. "There is wonderful material here, whether the setting be the earlier political struggle or the present-day political achievement." He admitted, however, that he had not yet read Bhattachara's *Music for Mohini*, which deals with this theme.

I asked Narayan about his writing methods. His answer applied only to his fiction, his weekly personal essay for the Sunday edition of the *Hindu* being produced more casually. "I can write best when I do not plan the subject too elaborately," he explained. "All my novels have been written in this manner. All I can settle for myself is my protagonist's general type of personality—my focus is all on character. If his personality comes alive, the rest is easy for me: background and minor characters develop as I progress." He elaborated later in a letter: "Each day I sit down to write, I feel curious about what may be coming out; only when the pen is actually running on am I able to think with precision. It probably means that I have to give my subconscious self a lot of freedom to work itself out. I try never to strain myself or force the pace."

Interest in method is strong among Indian writers, who have none of the aids of American authors—coaches, writers' conferences, textbooks, courses. That interest may explain at least in part Narayan's standing and the limited output of other talented men, like Raja Rao and Subhin Ghose, who have published only two books each. Although he tries to avoid all literary influences, Narayan's concentration on technique has led him in his time to study closely five authors, two of them Americans: Somerset Maugham, Graham Greene, Francois Mauriac, Sinclair Lewis, and John Steinbeck. He was especially impressed, he says, with *The Grapes of Wrath* and *Tortilla Flat*, which he calls "desirable patterns."

The Big Difference
Reprinted with permission from *The War Cry*, October 9, 1965.

From the magazines and newspapers issued by the Protestant churches we can get values that are not only of this world—but out of this world.

As Martin Marty has put it, we can—and often do—obtain the improper opinions, the views that are improper because they do not conform to the conventional beliefs that dominate our society.

Just how important this fact is can perhaps be best realized by thinking about the values in most Protestant-sponsored publications. Contrast them with the standards held up by most secular journalism. The emphases and the treatment clearly are different in the secular press.

The standard city and town newspaper, in the American journalistic tradition, reports and emphasizes all the ruptures in society. The bigger the conflict, the more prominent the news story about it. Secular journalism stresses differences and opposition, not reconciliation and healing. Labor-management disputes are reported on constantly, for instance, but labor-management harmony scarcely is noted. Editors and publishers generally believe that the news of violence and disorder sells more papers than news of order and decency. Selling more papers attracts more advertising. And more advertising means more income, a necessity for newspaper survival.

The secular press is remiss, not because it reports the news of conflict, which it must do if we are to know of its existence, but in the way it reports it: the place it has in the papers, the sizes of the headlines, the kinds of pictures.

The secular press insists that its philosophy is forced upon it by its need for survival economically, a need, it says, from which the church editor is free. With this excuse, all sorts of transgressions against the human spirit are committed. But it does help us to understand the pressures which the secular editor must face.

The secular newspaper, furthermore, has comparatively little interest in religion. Recall, for example, the concern for adequate coverage of sports in most of the 1,800 daily and 9,000 weekly papers of this nation. And what of religious news by comparison? Scattered here and there are little stories of meetings and new buildings, with now and then a big one if some major event occurs, such as an Ecumenical Council or a conflict within a denomination. Saturday may offer a church page, half of it advertising. Even so, this is improvement: religious news now appears on other pages any day and is receiving greater attention. But only at Christmas, Easter, Passover, or some other traditional religious time does religion rank with entertainment, sports, business and women's affairs.

In the eyes of a newspaper's city or managing editor religious or church news is "soft." "Hard" news is a juicy scandal, a strike, a big fire, and, of course, a war or some other international disaster. But church news is likely to be constructive and don't we all know that constructive news rarely sells many papers?

And where do editors place the blame for distorted emphasis? It is the fault, they say, of those of us who buy and read publications. We do not demand more or better-handled religious news. We, the people, clamor for whole pages on sports, business, and our other more intense interests than religion. We, the readers, are eager for detailed news of football, horse racing, or whatever sport is in season. We want stock reports down to the last digit and the news of the sexual adventures of actors. And this is true, if we can judge by circulation figures. Can we deny that the newspapers and magazines of the shallowest content have the biggest sales by far?

What would happen, however, if the usual standards of the church press were followed instead of the ordinary standards of the secular press? We have seen the difficulties in recent years of a church-published paper that does attempt this, and gets little support from the general public: the *Christian Science Monitor*. It has not succeeded in flourishing for several reasons, some of it its own doing, but one of which is that it is virtually alone in offering a religiously motivated general daily.

But if all members of the American Society of Newspaper Editors decided to give even the broad concept of religion its due, these editors might win more attention and be of more influence. But this they must do in unison.

A socially responsible press does not stop at giving the public what it wants. It also gives the public substantial and significant material which the owners of the press think the public might profit from having. And among such offerings could be better and more intelligent and intensive coverage of religious news and ideas.

The church publications of this country are not so timid as the secular publications on this score. They are not afraid to give the public something better than what it *seems* to want. Freed of the necessity to catch the attention of readers in direct competition, supported as most of them are by subsidies, and relatively independent of advertisers as compared with the secular publications, the best of Protestant publications report and comment on the world's news differently than the secular press.

It is the church press, not the secular press, that consistently tells the story of heroic missionary effort, of the rights of conscience in respect to war, of the rehabilitation of the mentally and physically ill.

It is the church press, not the secular, that has given support persistently to ways to help the aged, the sick, the crippled, the under-educated, the refugee and the dispossessed.

And it is the church press that has tried to tell a balanced, specific story of the church and of religion. Unlike the secular press, it has not been content with the blandness of the safe, general article or picture composed of symbols of all religions and faiths. It has taken sides, not always wisely or fairly, perhaps, but at least it let its readers know where it stands.

These, then, are all reasons why in these dangerous days the church member not only should support but also should read his church papers and magazines. The religious press is becoming, in the best sense of the word, a professional press. Technically some of its leaders are the equal of numerous secular publications. Some publications still are no more than lifeless house organs for a denomination or one of its departments, but these are losing ground in influence and significance to the publications with forthright and courageous opinions and writers producing articles far superior to what can be found in the majority of commercial journals in depth of comprehension and clarity of writing.

The church press can evaluate the world's events, the nation's policies, the actions of the people, from the standpoint of religion—a duty the secular press cannot perform. The press of the church can do this because it has the dynamics within it to exert such leaderships, and it has the dynamics because Christianity is at its center. The values of the Protestant religious press are not merely this world's values but also those of another world which must be reached in this one if man and society alike are to be saved. This is the big difference.

Why Freelancing Is Such Hard Work
Reprinted with permission from *Freelancer's Newsletter*, May 1, 1979.

John Braine, the novelist, once recalled meeting a businessman who asked him what his job was.

"I write," the author answered, as he recalled it in *Encounter*.

"I don't mean that," the businessman said. "I know that you've written a book. I mean what do you do for a living? What do you work at?"

Braine underscored that last sentence, as well he might, for it indicates an attitude frequently held toward writers.

It appears to be the view of the middle-aged as well as young people. One can understand it of youngsters like the little boy who once was my neighbor. He saw me trimming the lawn one mid-morning.

"Why aren't you at the office?" he asked me.

Before I could answer, his mother spared me the involved explanation. She told him I have an office in my home and do my work there as a writer when I'm not teaching at the university. Which indeed is true, despite the problem I had one year convincing the IRS that the room in which I write is genuinely an office, with three typewriters, two desks, a dozen vertical file drawers, and other appurtenances of a business, including that of writing.

But the middle-aged ought to know better. Not so the bus driver who let me off at my destination one noon. I had been up since six, working steadily except for breakfast and dressing to depart. As I left the bus he said sarcastically, "Starting a long day, I see."

We should not take it for granted that all people know how and when writers work, since it is the custom of most Americans at least to work fixed hours. But writers and other artists cannot always labor by the clock. Writers often stay in their offices from nine to twelve or one, and then stop for the day, especially if they are only part-timers. But their thinking processes do not end. H. L. Mencken used to write only in the evening, in his early days; Carl Van Doren said he worked no more than three or four hours at a time. And Somerset Maugham worked the nine to twelve shift; Conrad and Balzac used to spend a whole day just writing a sentence. This seems like lunacy, no doubt, to my bus driver friend.

How in the world can one spend a whole day on a sentence? But as all conscientious writers know, at times it is necessary. It may be a long sentence, loaded with meaning and dependent upon thorough assimilation of facts. Providing the situation for that sentence (especially in fiction) also consumes a great deal of time.

Once the sentence appears to have been perfected, which of course it is not in the opinions of most good writers—for they constantly see faults in their work—it must be fitted into context again. Then it must be allowed to cool, so that the writer can have a better perspective on the work. In half an hour the writer may have changed his or her mind, or as in journalism, someone else finds faults and the writer must start over.

Hard writing, goes the bromide, makes for easy reading. I often think that the reverse is true, too, especially when I read the quickly-spouted work of authors now having a little vogue; the murder-or-other-brutality-on-every-other-page novelists, or the let's-make-a-quick-grand-on-someone-else's-misery nonfiction writers.

Life Is Possible Without a Car
Reprinted with permission from *The Lookout*, 1981, The Standard Publishing Company.

My house is at the bottom of a block-long hill. If I go up to the top I can see two blocks of my street on one side and three on the other. Ours is a middle-class neighborhood and the only one without sidewalks. That lack makes the street look more exclusive than it really is.

Tree-lined, although not so thickly as a decade ago before the elms and maples were hit by diseases, the street has only one-family houses on it, four to ten on a side depending on the block length. Two exceptions are one side of a park and the edge of a woods.

One or two cars stand before all these houses or in garages, with three exceptions. Two of the three exceptions had cars until a few years ago; now the owners are too old to drive and have sold their vehicles.

The remaining exception is a couple who never have owned an automobile. Neither have this man and wife even operated one except for a few minutes behind the wheel years ago when a friend tried to interest them in becoming motorists.

What is life like for non-motorists in an America where the automobile has become—or is thought to be by car owners—as essential as water, heat and light? This carless couple can tell you, speaking only for a middle-class group. Being half of the pair, I have first-hand information.

We are a source of amazement to most strangers when they first learn of our odd, antediluvian condition. Their reactions are of two kinds: puzzlement that we have survived in U.S. society or congratulations on what they consider our common sense.

"But how do you get along? How do you get around?"

We explain that there is public transportation just a block from our house, a reliable bus line. For long trips we take planes, trains, buses. If it's raining hard we call a taxi, especially when there's no public transit connection. Friends sometimes take us along when they go marketing, although we rarely ask for lifts. The nearest supermarket is seven blocks away, a moderate walk with a wheeled shopping cart, although a bit slippery in winter, for our weather in that season is rigorous.

"How is it you've never had a car?"

That's another frequent question. Sometimes it is followed with "Don't you like cars?" "Do you get carsick?" both asked in the tone of voice used with "Don't you love your parents?"

It's not much of a mystery. We've always lived either near enough to where we worked so that we could walk to our offices or so far that public transport was more efficient and inexpensive than going by car.

Also, we've never had children. Our neighbors are busy taking theirs to schools, meetings, playgrounds, and other destinations so dear or necessary to youngsters. After a while their children want their own cars, so some neighbors have three. Two of these families include boys who like to buy wrecks and dismantle them, making their yards look like junk piles.

We'd gladly have bought and learned to run a car if we'd had the incentive of children. And now, no longer young, we do not trust our reflexes.

"You're sensible."

Sometimes this common observation is accompanied by the remarks of "you're saving a lot of money and avoiding a lot of trouble, what with taxes, repairs, gas, oil, and insurance costing more all the time. We really ought to do what you do."

Those who congratulate us, with the exception of one family, nevertheless stay loyal to their cars. The exception was a young couple with several children. They took to bicycles, buses, and, for heavy shopping, a cart with two large wheels.

Some people we know, on the other hand, instead of walking three blocks to a drugstore, drive there simply to buy a newspaper or a quart of ice cream. Car habits are hard to break.

We save money; we know that. We've asked friends to tell us how much they spend on their cars in a year, and the answers vary a lot. Even with our occasional use of taxicabs, our gifts of gasoline now and then to friends who take us in their cars, and our constant use of public transportation, we find that we spend less than half of what motorized life would require.

In addition there are certain satisfactions or results in being carless that drivers of autos may not know about.

We leave a parking space for others.

We do not endanger the lives of our fellow humans.

Our garage is a useful storage place denied us if we had to fill it with its intended occupant.

Our driveway lasts longer than if we had a car.

And we enjoy seeing old friends on the buses and making new ones on those journeys.

Religious Writers are Blockheads
Reprinted from *The Lutheran Companion*, March 8, 1961.

Religious writers are blockheads. Well, that's what the man said. Not exactly that way, of course, but that's what it amounts to. I don't say that I believe it, but that's what he said.

Who said it?

Sam Johnson

Sam Johnson?

Yes.

Who is he?

You know, the lexicographer. The famous Dr. Johnson, sometimes called "The Great Champ of Literature." Wrote for the *Gentlemen's* magazine and edited *The Rambler* (not the car, the periodical). Made James Boswell famous. Is buried in Westminster Abbey.

But what's this got to do with religious writing?

Lots. Dr. J. gave forth with this assertion in one of his famous conversations and it's been quoted ever since. He said: "No one but a blockhead ever wrote for anything but money."

And you believe it?

No, of course not. Not one little bit.

Why not?

Well, it's a long story. It goes back to one's basic philosophy. I won't say that Sam Johnson was crass or a fool all his life. I'm sure, though, that at the moment he uttered that silly, shallow sentence he was both. Unless he made a qualification, one which I'll make for him as we go along, but I can find no evidence that he ever did make it.

To begin with, it's not true. Thousands of people who definitely are not blockheads have written for rewards other than money.

Such as what?

Such as power, self-expression, the desire to be helpful, or to do good, influence, and even the wish to do evil. The other day, for instance, I came upon something written by John Gunther which he gave an organization that makes records for sightless people. I suppose Bernard Shaw never gave away a word free, but he was notorious for his grasping attitude and the world dislikes him for it.

And you find the altruistic spirit among religious writers?

Definitely. A number of editors of religious publications have told me of the prominent writers who got their start in their pages but who have never forgotten the fact and always have been grateful. Many of them are glad to submit stories and articles to minor publications that other writers ignore; other writers of their prominence, that is. Some will give away copy to those that cannot pay because they remember that they were treated kindly when they were beginners.

Not all, of course; editors also complain of writers whom they started on successful careers who now turn up their typewriters at them because their rates are comparatively low.

The main reason Dr. J. was wrong, of course, is that there is such a practice in the world of religion as stewardship. This principle is one which the religious writer, like any other religious person, should respect and take seriously. If he does, it means, of course, that he will gladly use his writing skill in behalf of his church or his denomination and not expect to be paid. Some writers refuse payment, in fact.

BUT—and this is a very big *but*: the church should not take advantage of this good will by paying everyone except the writer. If it pays the printer, the engraver, the U.S. post office, and the editors, it also should pay the writers. If it does not, it defeats the ideal of stewardship with injustice. And there are other qualifications: if the publication is out to make a profit, then certainly the religious writer should get his share—if he wants it. This is true whether the publication is issued by a church or by a commercial firm.

But back to Sam Johnson. In the world of religion we need lots of the kind of holy blockheads he talked about: people who write from some other motive than money-earning. Because with them we can continue to get out copy for church bulletins, parish papers, year books, denominational weeklies and monthlies, story papers, and various other religious publications.

They are glorious blockheads—for they are willing to put their skills at the service of an institution that needs their help. If you like, say they are willing to put their skills at the service of God. The church simply must be careful to appreciate them and not mistreat them.

Then religious writers are blockheads, after all? You seem to have argued yourself into accepting Sam Johnson's point.

Yes, in a way. But they are blessed blockheads, thank goodness. And we can't do without them.

Appendix 2

Students in Print

Visitors to my library always seem to be impressed by the special collection of books by my former students. Many journalism or English teachers could mount a similar display, so the visitors should not be so quick to give me credit. After all, I am only one of the many teachers these students had. What follows is only what I own by these writers. With few exceptions, each has published from one to as many as a dozen more.

Adeney, Miriam. *How to Write. God's Foreign Policy.*
Allen, Gina. *Forbidden Man. Rustics for Keeps.*
Anderson, Margaret J. *The Christian Writer's Handbook. Looking Ahead.*
Armstrong, Marjorie Moore. *School Someday. The Baptists in America* (with O.K. Armstrong).
Carty, James W. Jr. *The Gresham Years. Communicacion y Relaciones Publicas* (with Richardo Pastor Poppe). *Advertising the Local Church.*
Clay, Roberta. *The College Newspaper.*
Costa, Richard Hauer. *Edmund Wilson. H. G. Wells.*
Doyle, Lynne. *The Riddle of Genesis County.*
Eby, Omar. *How Full the River.*
Fensch, Thomas. *Steinbeck and Covici. Skydiving Book. Smokeys, Truckers, CB Radios & You.*
Fox, Rodney. *Agricultural and Technical Journalism.*
Grant, Joanne, ed., *Black Protest.*
Halter, Jon C. *Bill Bradley. Reggie Jackson. Their Backs to the Wall. Top Secret Projects of World War II.*
Hicks, Clifford B. *First Boy on the Moon. The Marvelous Inventions of Alvin Fernald. The Wacky World of Alvin Fernald.*
Hochstein, Rolaine. *Stepping Out. Table 47.*
Kent, Ruth K. *The Language of Journalism.*

Kern, Janet. *Yesterday's Child.*

Laubach, Robert S. *Toward World Literacy* (with Frank C. Laubach).

Lesly, Philip. *Public Relations Handbook.*

Lytel, Allen. *Microwave Test and Measurement Techniques.*

McDonald, Julie. *Amalie's Story. Petra. The Sailing Out. Ruth Buxton Sayre. Pathways to the Present.*

Mullins, Richard. *Most Valuable Player. Sound the Last Bugle.*

Owens, Loulie Latimer. *Minnie Belle. Saints of Clay.*

Patterson, Ronald (with Kyle Rote, Jr.). *Beyond the Goal.*

Paye, Anne. *Heritage of Faith.*

Phillips, Robert. *The Land of Lost Content.*

Pilarski, Laura. *They Came from Poland.*

Rivoyre, Christine de. *Morning Twilight. The Tangerine. Hansel et Gretel.*

Schneir, Walter and Miriam. *Invitation to an Inquest. Telling It Like It Was: The Chicago Riots* (eds).

Simon, Raymond, ed. *Perspectives in Public Relations.*

Simonsson, Bengt K. *The Way of the Word.*

Van Leeuwen, Jean. *Timothy's Flower.*

Wiebe, Katie Funk. *Good Times with Old Times.*

Yost, F. Donald. *Writing for Adventist Magazines.*

Index